Bond
No.1 for exam success

English

Assessment Papers

11+-12+ years

Book 2

OXFORD
UNIVERSITY PRESS

OXFORD
UNIVERSITY PRESS

Great Clarendon Street, Oxford, OX2 6DP, United Kingdom

Oxford University Press is a department of the University of Oxford.
It furthers the University's objective of excellence in research,
scholarship, and education by publishing worldwide. Oxford is a
registered trade mark of Oxford University Press in the UK and in
certain other countries

Text © Sarah Lindsay 2015
Original illustrations © Oxford University Press 2015

The moral rights of the authors have been asserted

First published in 2015

British Library Cataloguing in Publication Data
Data available

978-0-19-274008-3

10 9 8 7

Printed in Great Britain by Ashford Colour Press Ltd, Gosport, Hants

Acknowledgements

Illustrations: Nigel Kitching
Page make-up: GreenGate Publishing Services, Tonbridge, Kent
Cover illustrations: Lo Cole

The authors and publishers wish to thank the following for permission
to use copyright material: page 2 extract from 'The Little Grey Men' by
BB (D J Watkins-Pitchford), published by Methuen Children's Books ©
D J Watkins-Pitchford 1978; page 8 'The Overland Mail' by Rudyard
Kipling; page 14 extract from 'The Gamekeeper' by Barry Hines.
Reproduced with permission of Penguin Books 1975, 1979 © Barry Hines,
1975, 1979; page 21 extract from 'Hunter Davies' Lists', Octopus
Publishing Group 2004; page 27 extract from 'Animal Farm' by George
Orwell published by Penguin Books, © The Estate of Eric Blair 1945;
page 33 extract from 'Planet Earth' published by BBC Books 2006 ©
Alastair Fothergill (et al.); page 40 'APO 96225' by Larry Rottman, taken
from 'The Young Oxford Book of War Stories' by James Riordan,
originally from Perrine's Literature: Structure, Sound and Sense, 9th
edition by ARP/JOHNSON published by Heinle 2006; page 41 'Aftermath'
by Siegfried Sassoon, taken from www.bbc.co.uk/religion/remembrance/
poetry/wwone.shtml; page 47 article 'When government holds all the
cards' by Jeevan Vasagar. Reproduced with permission of The Guardian
© Guardian News & Media Ltd 2007; page 53 extract from 'As You Like It'
by William Shakespeare, taken from 'The Complete Works of William
Shakespeare, Compact Edition', edited by Wells, Stanley et al. (1988).
Reproduced with permission of OUP 1988; page 60 extract from 'Notes
from a Small Island' by Bill Bryson published by Doubleday/Transworld.

Although we have made every effort to trace and contact all
copyright holders before publication this has not been possible in all
cases. If notified, the publisher will rectify any errors or omissions at
the earliest opportunity.

Links to third party websites are provided by Oxford in good faith
and for information only. Oxford disclaims any responsibility for
the materials contained in any third party website referenced in
this work.

Before you get started

What is Bond?

This book is part of the Bond Assessment Papers series for English, which provides **thorough and continuous practice of key English skills** from ages five to thirteen. Bond's English resources are ideal preparation for many different kinds of tests and exams – from SATs to 11+ and other secondary school selection exams.

How does the scope of this book match real exam content?

English 11+–12+ Book 1 and Book 2 are the advanced Bond 11+ books. Each paper is **pitched a level above a typical 11+ exam**, providing greater challenge and stretching skills further. The papers practise comprehension, spelling, grammar and vocabulary work. They are also in line with other selective exams for this age group. The coverage supports the National Curriculum and the National Literacy Strategy and will also **provide invaluable preparation for higher level Key Stage 2 SATs performance**. It is outside the scope of this book to practise extended and creative writing skills. *Bond Focus on Writing* provides full coverage of writing skills.

What does the book contain?

- **10 papers** – each one contains 100 questions.

- **Tutorial links throughout** – – this icon appears in the margin next to the questions. It indicates links to the relevant section in *How to do 11+ English*, our invaluable subject guide that offers explanations and practice for all core question types.

- **Scoring devices** – there are score boxes in the margins and a Progress Chart on page 68. The chart is a visual and motivating way for children to see how they are doing. It also turns the score into a percentage that can help decide what to do next.

- **Next Step Planner** – advice on what to do after finishing the papers can be found on the inside back cover.

- **Answers** – located in an easily-removed central pull-out section.

How can you use this book?

One of the great strengths of Bond Assessment Papers is their flexibility. They can be used at home, in school and by tutors to:

- set **timed formal practice tests** – allow about 50 minutes per paper in line with standard 11+ demands. Reduce the suggested time limit by five minutes to practise working at speed

- provide **bite-sized chunks** for regular practice

- **highlight strengths and weaknesses** in the core skills

- identify **individual needs**

- set **homework**

- follow a **complete 11+ preparation strategy** alongside *The Parents' Guide to the 11+* (see below).

It is best to start at the beginning and work through the papers in order. If you are using the book as part of a careful run-in to the 11+, we suggest that you also have four other essential Bond resources close at hand:

How to do 11+ English: the subject guide that explains all the question types practised in this book. Use the cross-reference icons to find the relevant sections.

Focus on Comprehension: the practical handbook that clearly shows children how to read and understand the text, understand the questions and assess their own answers.

Focus on Writing: the essential resource that explains the key components of successful writing.

The Parents' Guide to the 11+: the step-by-step guide to the whole 11+ experience. It clearly explains the 11+ process, provides guidance on how to assess children, helps you to set complete action plans for practice and explains how you can use *English 11+–12+ Book 1 and Book 2* as part of a strategic run-in to the exam.

See the inside front cover for more details of these books.

What does a score mean and how can it be improved?

It is unfortunately impossible to guarantee that a child will pass the 11+ exam if they achieve a certain score on any practice book or paper. Success on the day depends on a host of factors, including the scores of the other children sitting the test. However, we can give some guidance on what a score indicates and how to improve it.

If children colour in the Progress Chart on page 68, this will give an idea of present performance in percentage terms. The Next Step Planner inside the back cover will help you to decide what to do next to help a child progress. It is always valuable to go over wrong answers with children. If they are having trouble with any particular question type, follow the tutorial links to *How To Do 11+ English* for step-by-step explanations and further practice.

Don't forget the website...!

Visit www.bond11plus.co.uk for lots of advice, information and suggestions on everything to do with Bond, the 11+ and helping children to do their best.

Key words

Some special words are used in this book. You will find them in **bold** each time they appear in the Papers. These words are explained here.

abbreviation	a word or words which is/are shortened
active verb	when the main person or thing does the action *he took it*
adjective	a word that describes somebody or something
adjectival phrase	a group of words describing a noun
adverb	a word that gives extra meaning to a verb
alphabetical order	words arranged in the order found in the alphabet
antonym	a word with a meaning opposite to another word *hot – cold*
clause	a section of a sentence with a verb
collective noun	a word referring to a group *swarm*
compound word	a word made up of two other words *football*
conditional	a clause or sentence expressing the idea that one thing depends on something else
conjunction	a word used to link sentences, phrases or words *and, but*
connective	a word or words that joins clauses or sentences
contraction	two words shortened into one with an apostrophe placed where the letter/s have been dropped *do not = don't*
definition	a meaning of a word
diminutive	a word implying smallness *booklet*
homophone	a word that has the same sound as another but a different meaning or spelling *right/write*
infinitive	the base form of a verb without any additional endings *clap*
metaphor	an expression in which something is described in terms usually associated with another *the sky is a sapphire sea*
mnemonic	a device to learn particular spellings *There is a rat in separate*
modal verb	used to help other words explain when something is necessary or possible *I can do my homework easily*
noun	a word for somebody or something
onomatopoeic	a word that echoes a sound, associated with its meaning *hiss*
passive verb	when the main person or thing has the action done to it *it was taken by him*
past tense	form of a verb showing that something has already happened
phrase	a group of words that act as a unit
plural	more than one *cats*
prefix	a group of letters added to the beginning of a word *un, dis*
preposition	a word that relates other words to each other *the book on the table*
pronoun	a word used to replace a noun *them*
root word	a word to which prefixes or suffixes can be added to make other words *quickly*
sentence	a unit of written language which makes sense by itself
simile	an expression to describe what something is like *as cold as ice*
singular	one *cat*
suffix	a group of letters added to the end of a word *ly, ful*
superlative	describes the limit of a quality (adjective or adverb) *most/least* or *shortest*
synonym	a word with the same or very similar meaning as another word *quick – fast*
verb	a 'doing' or 'being' word

The cool shadows across the forest path moved as the sun moved. A lovely tawny gold fritillary, newly hatched, came by, hovering over the bushes, passing on. Then a banded white admiral with gliding graceful flight. Man and dog slept; the sun, gathering power, made the moist fern steam. The hum of insects filled the air, the summer song of the woods. 5

Then the fern rustled and a face peeped out, a tiny bearded face, crowned by a batskin cap with the ears left on. It was Dodder.

There before him lay Giant Grum, all the hairy length of him, all the sweaty man-smell of him, fast asleep! This giant killed Otter, Otter of the gentle eyes, whose joy was the running water and spotted shingle. 10

The sides of the sleeping dog went in and out gently, the hind legs quivered in an uneasy dream, dream barks came from him and the half-opened eyes showed white with sleep. Dodder moved through the fern to where the heavy gun lay among the crushed bracken fronds. A ladybird was crawling up the blued barrel. It reached the end and wavered uncertainly. Then a bumble bee came droning 15 through the fern forest. It found the head of a purple knapweed and clambered on it, bending it right over until it touched the gun stock. Dodder saw the polished grain of the wood and the worn smooth appearance of the steel barrel where the giant's sweaty hand held it when firing.

He put his fingers into his pocket and drew forth the leaves, the six oak leaves 20 which Pan had given him. He crept to the muzzle of the gun.

*   *   *

A tiny pine twig dropped from the tree above. It struck the giant on the nose and he sat up stretching.

Ah! he felt better – that terrible ennui had left him. Nothing like a nap in the open air. The dog was still asleep. What had awakened him? He scratched his nose and 25 looked about him. This would never do. Supposing his master had caught him sleeping, he might get the sack!

Ah! What was that he had been dreaming, something about his pheasant pens. He chuckled, what silly things are dreams!

Pat! Another stick fell. He looked up into the tangled dark branches above him. 30 A squirrel was it… something. He got to his feet, peering up, his sharp eyes searching, searching. And then he saw Dodder, perched on a branch thirty feet above him. The dog was awake too, the hairs bristling along the ridge of its back, its eyes staring upwards.

*   *   *

Giant Grum groaned and passed his hands over his eyes. Oh dear, still seeing 35 things! He looked again. Yes… yes… a tiny man in a batskin cap and coat sitting on a pine branch. Beside him was a grey squirrel.

But these things *can't* be; after all, one must be practical. The squirrel, yes… but that other thing… there weren't such things as gnomes… it was impossible. It must be a new kind of bat! And then, as he watched, the vulgar little gnome leaned 40 forward and spat! The tiny spot of white came swiftly down like a plummet and hit him in the eye. Giant Grum let out an oath.

*   *   *

The gun came up, a cracked finger with a black nail crooked round the trigger. A gnome was it! Well, we would see! Neither Dodder nor Squirrel moved, the tiny face was actually grinning at him.   45

Giant Grum's right thumb pushed forward the catch on the top of the gun, hiding the one tiny word 'safe'. He pressed the trigger and then… something went 'pouf' at the giant, blowing him out like a candle.

'It was simple,' said Dodder to an admiring ring of animals who had gathered round Tree Top House.   50

'I pushed the leaves down inside each barrel, and then Squirrel and I went up the tree. He was fast asleep and we threw things on him to wake him. Then he stood up and aimed his club that roars. I knew Pan was with me, I wasn't afraid when I saw those two black mouths pointing at me, I knew the leaves would burst the gun. Then he fired, there was a great noise and the giant went backwards into the   55
bracken. I think he was dead; I was glad to come away. Listen!'

And then they heard birds singing; blackbirds, thrushes, willow warblers, wood wrens, blackcaps, white throats, tits, chaffinches, greenfinches, and the glorious voice of the nightingales. The birds had come back to Crow Wood at last!

From The Little Grey Men by BB (DJ Watkins-Pitchford)

Answer these questions.

1 What is casting the shadows in the forest (line 1)?

_____

2 Who was Giant Grum's companion? _____

3–4 In your own words describe how Dodder felt about Giant Grum and why.

_____

_____

_____

5 Which **phrase** in the passage tells us the Giant's gun was well used?

_____

6–7 How many oak leaves had Pan given Dodder? What were they used for?

_____

_____

8 What does the word 'banded' mean (line 3)? _____

9–11 Throughout the passage the author occasionally stops the story and then starts again, jumping forward in time. In your own words, reflecting the author's style, fill the gap in time between line 48 and line 51 ('blowing him out like a candle…' 'I pushed the leaves down inside').

_____

_____

_____

_____

_____

12 How do we know there are more important giants than Giant Grum?

_____

13–14 Does the giant have good or bad eyesight? Use evidence from the passage to support your answer.

_____

_____

15 Why did Giant Grum think he was seeing things?

_____

_____

16 Copy the **phrase** that Dodder uses to describe the gun.

_____

17 What returned to the woods now Grum was dead?

_____

18–20 How would you describe Dodder, as shown in this passage? Use two pieces of evidence from the passage to support your answer.

_____

_____

_____

_____

_____

_____

20

Write two words using each of the **prefixes**.

E 2

21–22 tele- _____   _____

23–24 sub- _____   _____

25–26 con- _____   _____

6

Write an *ough* word that rhymes with each of these words.

E 2

27 tough _____   **28** nought _____

29 thorough _____   **30** dough _____

31 bough _____

5

Underline the **preposition** in each **sentence**.

D 6

32 Fran was miserable, she felt at her wits' end.

33 The explorer struggled through the opening.

34 Jake's younger brother went down on all fours when wapretending to be a cat.

3

Put these words in reverse **alphabetical order**.

E 2

preference   **prefabricate**   **preferment**   **preferable**   **preferential**

35 (1) _____   **36** (2) _____

37 (3) _____   **38** (4) _____

39 (5) _____

5

Complete each of these **sentences** with two additional **clauses**. Underline each **clause**.

D 2

40 Yousef went _____

_____

41 The fierce dog _____

_____

42 The autumn leaves _____

_____

43 Kitty spoke sternly _____

_____

44 Danny didn't appreciate _____

_____

45 Our teacher _____

_____

6

D 6

Form a **noun** from each of the **verbs**.

46 dramatise   There was a standing ovation at the end of the _____.

47 reject   The elderly cat felt an overwhelming sense of _____ once the kitten arrived.

48 govern   The _____ introduced many new laws.

49 supply   The local _____ failed to deliver on time.

50 terrorise   Meena felt _____ as the snarling dog moved closer.

51 expend   The holiday was a huge _____.

6

E 2

Write a **simile** using each of the words in bold.

52 cucumber   _____

53 feather   _____

54 duck   _____

55 dodo   _____

56 March hare   _____

57 fiddle   _____

6

E 2

Fill in the missing letter in each word.

58 excep__ion   **59** ambi__ion   **60** transfu__ion

61 crucifi__ion   **62** dissua__ion   **63** convec__ion

64 eleva__ion   **65** comple__ion   **66** conver__ion

9

Copy and add the missing punctuation to the following.

67–79 the icy wind froze petra to the core the forest giving little protection against the increasing snowfall

we must find shelter soon she yelled to tom or we will never make it to morning

_____

_____

_____

_____

_____

_____

D 5

13

Identify the part of speech of each of the words in bold.

D 6

         (80)   (81)   (82)
It was the **scariest**, **darkest**-looking place. The huge stone **walls** were

   (83)   (84)   (85)
entwined with leafless stems **of** wisteria and in patches, suffocated **with** ivy.

80 _____

81 _____

82 _____

83 _____

84 _____

85 _____

6

Write each **contraction** in full.

D 5

86 could've   _____

87 shan't   _____

88 won't   _____

89 they'll   _____

4

Write two **definitions** for this word. One might be a meaning that has evolved over recent years.

E 2

90–91 web

(1) _____

(2) _____

2

Write three words that use the **root word** in bold.

92–94 **connect** _____ _____ _____

95–97 **sense** _____ _____ _____

98–100 **happy** _____ _____ _____

9

Now go to the Progress Chart to record your score! Total 100

Paper 2

The Overland Mail
(Foot-Service to the Hills)

In the name of the Empress of India, make way,
    O Lords of the Jungle, wherever you roam.
The woods are astir at the close of the day –
    We exiles are waiting for letters from Home.
Let the robber retreat – let the tiger turn tail –   5
In the Name of the Empress, the Overland Mail!

With a jingle of bells as the dusk gathers in,
    He turns to the foot-path that heads up the hill –
The bags on his back and a cloth round his chin,
    And, tucked in his waist-belt, the Post Office bill: 10
"Despatched on this date, as received by the rail,
Per runner, two bags of the Overland Mail."

Is the torrent in spate? He must ford it or swim.
    Has the rain wrecked the road? He must climb by the cliff.
Does the tempest cry "Halt"? What are tempests to him?   15
    The Service admits not a "but" or an "if."
While the breath's in his mouth, he must bear without fail,
In the Name of the Empress, the Overland Mail.

From aloe to rose-oak, from rose-oak to fir,
    From level to upland, from upland to crest,   20
From rice-field to rock-ridge, from rock-ridge to spur,
    Fly the soft sandalled feet, strains the brawny brown chest.
From rail to ravine – to the peak from the vale –
Up, up through the night goes the Overland Mail.

There's a speck on the hillside, a dot on the road –   25
    A jingle of bells on the foot-path below –
There's a scuffle above in the monkey's abode –
    The world is awake, and the clouds are aglow.
For the great Sun himself must attend to the hail:
"In the name of the Empress the Overland Mail!"   30

by Rudyard Kipling

Answer these questions.

  1 Where does the poem take place?

_____

  2 In whose name is the mail carried?

_____

  3 What is meant by the **phrase** 'the woods are astir' (line 3)?

_____

_____

  4 Explain what is meant by the **phrase** 'the Overland Mail'.

_____

5 Copy the line from the poem that explains how the mail carrier physically carries the mail.

_____

_____

6 How is the mail brought to the mail carrier? _____

7–9 What are three physical difficulties the mail carrier must overcome?

_____

_____

_____

10–11 At what time of day does the poem begin? Use one piece of evidence from the poem to support your answer.

_____

_____

12–13 At what time of day does the poem end? Use one piece of evidence from the poem to support your answer.

_____

_____

14–16 Write a **definition** for each of these words.

retreat (line 5): _____

ravine (line 23): _____

abode (line 27): _____

17 What is meant by the **phrase** 'The Service admits not a "but" or an "if"' (line 16)?

_____

_____

18 Which **phrase** or line in the poem suggests that the mail carrier believes it is his duty to deliver the mail?

_____

_____

19 Explain what the **phrase** 'Fly the soft sandalled feet' means (line 22).

_____

20 In your own words, explain what the poem is about.

_____

_____

_____

Underline the **verbs** in the **sentences**.

21 She walked slowly to school.

22 For the first time he looked Hannah in the eye.

23–24 The ship sank back down and disappeared forever.

25–27 Niall had come to a halt outside the shop window, but a crowd rushed past and hurried him on.

Use the listed **homophones** correctly, in a **sentence**.

28–29 dual   duel

_____

30–31 whose   who's

_____

32–33 council   counsel

_____

34–35 draft   draught

_____

Circle any of these words which should always start with a capital letter.

36–40 umbrella   elizabeth   picnic   victorian   examination   pilot

cardiff   new guinea   shakespeare   number   microwave

Write four **compound** adjectives.

41–44 _____   _____   _____   _____

Complete these **proverbs**.

45 Better _____ never.

46 Blood _____ water.

47 Every _____ lining.

48 A _____ thoughts.

49 More _____ speed.

50 Many _____ work.

D 1

6

Write the following in their **plural** form.

E 2

51 class	_____	**52** series	_____
53 ellipsis	_____	**54** kilo	_____
55 chief	_____	**56** cactus	_____
57 trout	_____	**58** elf	_____

8

Rewrite these **sentences** changing them from **singular** to **plural**.

E 2

59–61 The bird sang in the tree near the fountain.

_____

62–65 She won a ticket to watch a local comedian perform.

_____

66–68 The child was splashing the elderly swimmer.

_____

10

Write an **antonym** for each of these words.

D 9

69 extinct	_____	**70** frozen	_____
71 friend	_____	**72** envelop	_____
73 occupied	_____	**74** narrow	_____
75 glance	_____	**76** cruel	_____
77 augment	_____	**78** developed	_____

10

Write the following using indirect speech.

79–82 Ben asked, "Is it time for lunch? I'm starving."

"Let's sit on the beach, then we can feed the seagulls," replied Tariq.

Ben asked _____ as

_____.

Tariq suggested _____ so

_____.

D 12

4

E 2

Match the words with their **definitions**. Write the correct number in the space.

83 indicate	_____	(1) native	
84 individual	_____	(2) essential	
85 indomitable	_____	(3) to make known	
86 induce	_____	(4) hard-working	
87 industrious	_____	(5) unconcerned	
88 indifferent	_____	(6) separate	
89 indispensable	_____	(7) to persuade	
90 indigenous	_____	(8) stubbornly persistent	

8

D 6

Underline the **conjunction** in each line.

91 therefore   don't   hiss   they   separate   exceptional

92 will   all   while   swarm   them   least

93 breeze   second   intense   was   sad   as

3

E 2

Complete the following words with *ie* or *ei*.

94 p_____ce   **95** bes_____ge   **96** dec_____t

97 w_____rd   **98** rev_____w   **99** exper_____nce

100 anc_____nt

7

The gamekeeper finished his meal with a cup of tea and two biscuits, then he went
outside in his shirt-sleeves. The sun was still up, the trees filtered the breeze, and
the air was still warm in the yard...

John and Ian walked up the yard carrying sacks. The gamekeeper followed them
carrying a landing net. He started to whistle as he approached the pen so that the   5
pheasants would know who was coming, and he carried on whistling as they went
inside and he closed the door behind them. But the pheasants were still alarmed
at the presence of three people; they were used to seeing the gamekeeper on his
own. They ran for the corners, and hid under the tents of evergreen propped up
against the sides of the pen. The boys stood still waiting for their father to tell them   10
what to do.

'I'll catch them, then you can take turns holding them while I take the brails off. All right?'
John nodded. Ian put his sacks down and sat on them.
'Can't we catch any, Dad?'
'No, you'll be running up and down frightening them to death.'   15
'Why will we?'
'I know you. We'll finish up with a stampede on our hands and a penful of
nervous wrecks.'
'We'll not.'
'I'll send you out if you don't stop arguing, Ian.'   20
'It's not right, Dad.'
He sat with his head down, then scuffed a pheasant dropping into the earth
with his plimsoll, as though it was something poisonous which had started to
crawl towards him.
'All right then, I'll let you catch the last two if you behave yourselves and do as   25
you are told.'
The gamekeeper selected a hen pheasant and walked towards it, holding the net
at the ready. He could have been advancing on a butterfly. The pheasant ran to the
end of the pen, then turned into a corner, and by quickly following up and feinting
to right and left, whichever way the bird threatened to escape, the gamekeeper was   30
able to get close enough to reach out with the handle and pop the net over the
bird. It struggled, its feet became enmeshed and the gamekeeper held it down until
John was kneeling by the bird; then he turned the handle to let the boy free the
pheasant. He stood up with it, and held it still, speaking gently to it while his father
felt amongst the feathers of the left wing and pulled out the paper fastener which   35
secured the leather brail. The wing was free now. The bird could fly again. He gave
the wing back to John to fold close to its body, so that it could not flap it, which
might panic it and injure it in a struggle.
John carried it to the door of the pen, opened it, and put the pheasant down
outside. It ran across the clearing, then disappeared amongst the trees, leaving a   40
faint slipstream behind it in the grass.
It was Ian's turn next to release the pheasant from the net and hold it while his
father unfastened the brail. It ran under one of the evergreen hides.
'Go to the other end, Ian, and make it come back this way. But don't bend down
and pop your face in there, I don't want it dying of fright.'   45

If John had been there on his own, the gamekeeper would have let him unfasten the brails. But not with them both helping. Ian would have caused aggravation if he could not have unfastened some, and it would have taken him too long to have undone them on his own.

When they had released half of the pheasants through the pen door, they 50
captured the rest and placed them in the sacks, six or seven to a sack, ready to be loaded into the back of the gamekeeper's van, to be released in other coverts on his beat…

The sun had gone by the time they had loaded the last sack of pheasants into the van… The boys went in for bed, and the gamekeeper drove quickly up the track 55
towards the main road. He was in a hurry. He wanted to release the pheasants before it got dark, so that they would have time to find a safe roosting place for the night.

He emptied the sacks in Boundary Wood, and in a spinney called the Willowgarth. He placed the last sack on the ground near a hedge which separated the trees from the fields, and began to twitch the bottom, at the same time tipping 60
the sack gently to encourage the pheasants out. A cock was first out. It ran through the hedge into the field and took off. It had to work hard to gain elevation…

At the bottom of the field, two men with two dogs were kneeling by some reeds at the edge of a pond. They had heard the whirring and clapping of the pheasant's wings as it took off, and had ducked down, hoping that it would not see them, and 65
that it might land near enough for them to sneak up on it and let the dogs have a run at it.

From *The Gamekeeper* by Barry Hines

Answer these questions.

1 At what time of day is this passage set? _____

2 Why did the gamekeeper whistle as he approached the pheasants?

_____

_____

3 Who was John and Ian's father? _____

4 Explain what is meant by 'We'll finish up with a stampede on our hands and a penful of nervous wrecks' (lines 17–18).

_____

_____

5–6 Describe in your own words how the gamekeeper caught the hen pheasant.

_____

_____

7 What is the meaning of the word 'feinting' on line 29?

_____

8 Write a synonym for the word 'enmeshed' (line 32). _____

9 What are the brails used for?

_____

10–12 Which boy do you think is the younger? Give two reasons.

_____

_____

_____

_____

13–16 Using evidence from the passage, describe each of the boys' characters.

_____

_____

_____

_____

_____

_____

_____

17 Why do you think the cock 'had to work hard to gain elevation' (line 62)?

_____

_____

_____

18 What were the intentions of the men in the final paragraph?

_____

_____

19–20 The gamekeeper later notices the two men. How do you think this would have made him feel? What do you think he did? Explain why.

_____

_____

_____

_____

_____

_____

◯ 20

E 2

Underline the unstressed vowels in each word. There could be more than one.

21 nursery **22** camera **23** valuable

24 strawberry **25** vegetable **26** interest

27–29 Write three more words that contain unstressed vowels.

_____   _____   _____

◯ 9

D 13

Rewrite these **sentences**, eliminating the double negatives.

30 There weren't no dolphins swimming by the boat.

_____

31 Daniel didn't play in no football match.

_____

32 The spelling test wasn't not very hard this week.

_____

33 Denholm didn't want no piano lesson.

_____

34 Alex wasn't not late for school.

_____

35 Mr Thomas hadn't caught no fish after three hours!

_____

◯ 6

Fill the gap by writing the **past tense** of the **verb** in bold.

D 6

36 to weep   Sam _____ when the kitten died.

37 to throw   Ian _____ the ball over the wall.

38 to write   They _____ long, imaginative stories.

39 to be   Meena _____ very tired after her late night.

40 to have   The Kingston family _____ a fantastic holiday.

5

Write five words which are of common gender.

D 8

41–45 _____   _____   _____

_____   _____

5

Circle the **pronouns** in this passage.

D 6

46–54 It looked up at them with sad, droopy eyes. How could they consider leaving him? They bundled the shivering dog into the blanket to keep him warm. She wouldn't have to know who had taken him!

9

Write seven **contractions** which incorporate the words in bold.

D 5

shall   would   I   have   will   not

55–61 _____   _____   _____

_____   _____   _____

_____

7

Rewrite the **phrases** below in more formal English.

D 2

62 Don't give me that old rubbish.

_____

63 Get a life.

_____

2

Write the following as **abbreviations**.

D 10

64 south west _____

65 Bachelor of Education _____

66 brothers _____

67 read-only memory _____

68 square metre _____

69 company _____

70 His Royal Highness _____

71 and so forth _____

8

D 4

Rewrite the passage adding the missing commas.

72–75 My mum spends hours making all our presents. She makes candlesticks that look like trees biscuit barrels that look like dog kennels water-bottle-holders that attach to your arm and many other unusual gifts. Most people love the presents showing them off to friends and neighbours. However sometimes you can tell they aren't very pleased!

_____

_____

_____

_____

_____

_____

_____

4

Add the **suffix** ous to each of these words. Remember to make any necessary spelling changes.

E 2

76 humour _____ 77 courage _____

78 rebel _____ 79 prestige _____

80 gas _____ 81 nutrition _____

82 caution _____ 83 grace _____

8

Complete the table by writing in words that have 3, 4 or 5 syllables.

84–91

No. of syllables	Word		
3	*extremely*		
4			
5			

Write three **compound words** incorporating each of the words listed.

92–94 any   _____   _____   _____

95–97 hand   _____   _____   _____

98–100 time   _____   _____   _____

8

9

Now go to the Progress Chart to record your score!   Total   100

Who invented what

Things are rarely invented just like that, out of the blue, with nothing or no-one having
gone before, working along a similar path. And very often when the breakthrough
comes, it's a team effort. Sometimes no-one knows the inventor, the original begetter
never having been acknowledged, especially when the invention was a long time ago.

Here are some everyday, domestic objects in constant use, which we all roughly   *5*
take for granted, with their probable origins.

Inventions that turn out to be incredibly ancient

1 **Glass, 2500BC:** Could have been discovered by accident, when sand got heated
   with limestone and wood ash. Small glass ornamental beads have been found
   dating back to 2500BC, but it was the Egyptians around 1450BC who developed   *10*
   other uses, such as glass bottles.
2 **Locks, 2000BC:** The Egyptians used a wooden bolt held tight by pins dropped
   into holes – only a key shaped to push all the pins out of the way could open it.
   Much like locks today, really.
3 **Socks, 800BC:** The first wearers are not known, but presumably when we   *15*
   gave up bare feet for shoes of some sort, socks of some sort came in. The first
   mention of them was in a poem by the Greek poet Hesiod around 700BC. They
   were bits of felt at first, patched together. Knitted socks were created by the
   Egyptians around 450BC.
4 **Metal coins, 600BC:** People often exchanged a piece of precious metal for   *20*
   goods, but there was no standardised exchange value and it was hard to weigh
   and evaluate worth. The first known standardised coins, all weighing the same,
   and stamped with the king's head, were issued around 600BC by the Lydians in
   what is now western Turkey.

Remarkably oldish inventions

1 Spectacles, 1280AD: A pair of glass lenses, clipped onto the nose, were first noted in the 13th century, but no inventor was credited. Spectacle-making was known in Florence from 1301 where Alessandro de Spina and Salvino degli Armatti were credited with inventing them. On the other hand, the Chinese say they got there first around 900AD.

2 Watches, 1500: Sundials or shadow clocks used to tell the time date from 3500. The origin of mechanical clocks, fitted into towers, is unknown, but the first striking clock was erected in Milan in 1335. Salisbury Cathedral had one from 1386 – it still works. Watches, which could be carried around, were invented by Peter Henlein, a German locksmith, in 1500. The original was about the size of a large mobile phone and was carried by hand.

3 Pencil, 1565: Invented by Conrad Gesner, a German-Swiss who realised the potential of graphite and encased it in a wooden holder to form a means of writing.

4 Flush lavatory, 1591: John Harrington, an Elizabethan courtier, installed the first recorded one at Richmond Palace.

Dead-modern inventions

1 Jeans, 1873: During the Gold Rush in the USA, Levi Strauss Co. supplied prospectors with materials and clothes, including trousers. A tailor called Jacob Davis suggested that trousers made of denim – a material that had originated from Nimes in France, hence de Nimes – complete with riveted pockets, would go down well. And they did. In 1873 Strauss registered the first patent for jeans.

2 Toothpaste,1896: As we know it, coming out of a tube, toothpaste was introduced by William Colgate in 1896. Before that it had been packaged in jars. It was tried in a tube in 1892 by another American, Washington Sheffield, but it didn't quite work. Colgate developed the tube nozzle so that the toothpaste, as it boasted on the side of the tube, 'comes out a ribbon, lies flat on the brush'.

3 Mobile phone, 1970: Pioneered in the USA by Bell Laboratories, they had a trial run in Chicago in 1979 and opened their first public service in 1983, but meanwhile the Scandinavians had got in first, launching their own system in 1981.

4 World Wide Web, 1989: Created by English physicist Tim Berners-Lee while working for the European Centre for Nuclear Research in Switzerland. He needed to get information into computers scattered across the world; he defined the system, wrote the software, then passed it on to the world, for nothing. Thanks, Tim.

From Hunter Davies' Lists

Answer these questions.

1 What is the meaning of the word 'begetter' as used in the passage in line 3?

_____

2 Which ancient group appear to have developed many early inventions?

_____

3 How is it believed glass was discovered?

_____

4–5 Give two reasons why we do not have the names of the actual inventors for the earliest inventions.

_____

_____

6 What is meant by 'standardised exchange value' (line 21)?

_____

7 What is special about the clock in Salisbury Cathedral?

_____

8 In what way have watches improved over time?

_____

9 What are pencils made from?

_____

10 Which historical period covered the 1590s? _____

11 What is the origin of the word 'denim' when referring to denim jeans?

_____

_____

12–13 Choose one 'dead-modern' invention listed in the passage and describe it in as few words as possible.

_____

_____

_____

14–16 Give three reasons why the invention of the World Wide Web has been so important for society today.

_____

_____

_____

_____

17 Why was Tim Berners-Lee's invention so selfless?

_____

18–20 Of all the inventions listed, which would you say has had the biggest impact on your life? Give three reasons why.

_____

_____

_____

_____

_____ 20

Sort these words into the following parts of speech.

D 6

| kneeling | by | two | run | they | with | it | enthusiastic |

21–22 verbs _____ _____

23–24 adjectives _____ _____

25–26 pronouns _____ _____

27–28 prepositions _____ _____ 8

Rewrite the passage below, adding the missing punctuation. Start new lines where necessary.

D 5

29–51 Go back to your lesson said Mrs Patel and let me hear no more about it But… began Sam Mrs Patel leaned forward I mean it she said with menace I'll go Sam replied and entered the classroom with her head bowed

_____

_____

_____

_____

_____

_____

_____

_____ 23

Add *cial* or *tial* to complete each word correctly.

52 benefi_____

53 essen_____

54 influen_____

55 superfi_____

56 ini_____

57 prejudi_____

Some of the following pairs of words are **synonyms** and some are **antonyms**. Put them in the table in the correct column.

58–65

foreseen/expected   fortunate/unlucky   knightly/magnanimous

liberal/conservative   appalling/appealing   plethora/abundance

grand/dignified   demolish/retain

Synonyms	Antonyms

Improve these **sentences** by changing the group of words in bold for a single one.

66 The young boy sang along to the radio, getting the **words to the song** wrong, much to the delight of his older brother.

_____

67 My mum kept her great-grandfather's war diaries for **the interest of future generations**.

_____

68 The **bowl filled with lettuce, tomatoes and dressing** was delicious!

_____

69 The **official count of the people** showed that more babies were being born.

_____

70 Theo's **humorous name for a person** was Lightning because he was such a fast runner.

_____

5

To each **verb** add an **adverb** that could describe it.

71 was _____   72 pack _____

73 supped _____   74 wangle _____

75 threw _____   76 swung _____

77 forgot _____   78 holler _____

D 6
8

Place a semi-colon in each of these **sentences**.

D 5

79 The ground beneath our feet began to shake, red wheels roared through clouds of steam they were pulling tanks, guns and ammunition.

80 The question won't be pushed to the back of my mind on the contrary it fills my every waking moment.

81 The water doesn't run properly, only a trickle the cupboards are bare, apart from half a packet of stale biscuits.

82 Ling Sung practises his piano very hard Raj doesn't practise and is still the best!

4

Match these words with their meanings. Write the number of the correct **definition** by each word.

E 2

(1) not genuine or authentic
(2) active, nimble
(3) to reject scornfully
(4) neat and trim in appearance
(5) a small branch
(6) dirty and unpleasant

83 spurn _____   84 sprig _____

85 spruce _____   86 spurious _____

87 squalid _____   88 spry _____

6

Add a different **clause** to each of these to make a longer **sentence**.

D 2

89 The wind blew relentlessly _____

_____

90 The wind blew relentlessly _____

_____

91 The wind blew relentlessly _____

_____

3

Next to each word, state where you think it came from (for example, from another language or the name of a person).

92 meow _____

93 spaghetti _____

94 hoover _____

Spell each of these words correctly.

95 prefered _____   **96** nuisence _____

97 apparant _____   **98** imediately _____

99 disatous _____   **100** consciance _____

Now go to the Progress Chart to record your score!   Total   100

Paper 5

Now, as it turned out, the Rebellion was achieved much earlier and more easily than anyone had expected. In past years Mr Jones, although a hard master, had been a capable farmer, but of late he had fallen on evil days. He had become much disheartened after losing money in a lawsuit, and had taken to drinking more than was good for him. For whole days at a time he would lounge in his Windsor chair 5
in the kitchen, reading the newspapers, drinking and occasionally feeding Moses on crusts of bread soaked in beer. His men were idle and dishonest, the fields were full of weeds, the buildings wanted roofing, the hedges were neglected, and the animals were underfed.

June came and the hay was almost ready for cutting. On Midsummer's Eve, 10
which was a Saturday, Mr Jones went into Willingdon and got so drunk at the Red Lion that he did not come back till midday on Sunday. The men had milked the cows in the early morning and then had gone out rabbiting, without bothering to feed the animals. When Mr Jones got back he immediately went to sleep on the drawing-room sofa with the *News of the World* over his face, so that when evening 15
came, the animals were still unfed. At last they could stand it no longer. One of the cows broke in the door of the store-shed with her horns and all the animals began to help themselves from the bins. It was just then that Mr Jones woke up. The next moment he and his four men were in the store-shed with whips in their hands, lashing out in all directions. This was more than the hungry animals could 20
bear. With one accord, though nothing of the kind had been planned beforehand,

they flung themselves upon their tormentors. Jones and his men suddenly found themselves being butted and kicked from all sides. The situation was quite out of their control. They had never seen animals behave like this before, and this sudden uprising of creatures whom they were used to thrashing and maltreating just as they chose, frightened them almost out of their wits. After only a moment or two they gave up trying to defend themselves and took to their heels. A minute later all five of them were in full flight down the cart-track that led to the main road, with the animals pursuing them in triumph.

Mrs Jones looked out of the bedroom window, saw what was happening, hurriedly flung a few possessions into a carpet bag, and slipped out of the farm by another way. Moses sprang off his perch and flapped after her, croaking loudly. Meanwhile the animals had chased Jones and his men out on to the road and slammed the five-barred gate behind them. And so, almost before they knew what was happening, the Rebellion had been successfully carried through: Jones was expelled, and the Manor Farm was theirs.

For the first few minutes the animals could hardly believe in their good fortune. Their first act was to gallop in a body right round the boundaries of the farm, as though to make quite sure that no human being was hiding anywhere upon it; then they raced back to the farm buildings to wipe out the last traces of Jones's hated reign. The harness-room at the end of the stables was broken open; the bits, the nose-rings, the dog-chains, the cruel knives with which Mr Jones had been used to castrate the pigs and lambs, were all flung down the well. The reins, the halters, the blinkers, the degrading nosebags, were thrown on to the rubbish fire which was burning in the yard. So were the whips. All the animals capered with joy when they saw the whips going up in flames. Snowball also threw on to the fire the ribbons with which the horses' manes and tails had usually been decorated on market days.

'Ribbons,' he said, 'should be considered as clothes, which are the mark of a human being. All animals should go naked.'

When Boxer heard this he fetched the small straw hat which he wore in summer to keep the flies out of his ears, and flung it on to the fire with the rest.

In a very little while the animals had destroyed everything that reminded them of Mr Jones. Napoleon then led them back to the store-shed and served out a double ration of corn to everybody, with two biscuits for each dog. Then they sang 'Beasts of England' from end to end seven times running, and after that they settled down for the night and slept as they had never slept before.

But they woke at dawn as usual, and suddenly remembering the glorious thing that had happened, they all raced out into the pasture together. A little way down the pasture there was a knoll that commanded a view of most of the farm. The animals rushed to the top of it and gazed round them in the clear morning light. Yes, it was theirs – everything that they could see was theirs! In the ecstasy of that thought they gambolled round and round, they hurled themselves into the air in great leaps of excitement. They rolled in the dew, they cropped mouthfuls of the sweet summer grass, they kicked up clods of the black earth and snuffed its rich scent. Then they made a tour of inspection of the whole farm and surveyed with speechless admiration the ploughland, the hayfield, the orchard, the pool, the spinney. It was as though they had never seen these things before, and even now they could hardly believe that it was all their own.

From *Animal Farm* by George Orwell

Answer these questions.

1–2 Why had Mr Jones 'fallen on evil days' (line 3)?

_____

_____

3 Which statement tells you a rebellion had been planned by the animals?

_____

_____

4–5 Give two reasons why the animals felt the need for rebellion.

_____

_____

_____

6 What does the **phrase** 'with one accord' mean (line 21)?

_____

7 At what time of year did the rebellion take place?

_____

8 What made the animals rebel on this particular day?

_____

9–10 How would you describe the sort of person Mr Jones is, as shown in the passage? Use an example from the passage to support your answer.

_____

_____

_____

_____

11 How many men worked for Mr Jones? _____

12–13 Describe in your own words how Mr Jones and his men felt when the animals turned against them. Use evidence from the passage to support your answer.

_____

_____

_____

_____

14 What type of animal is Moses? _____

15 Why did the animals first race round the farm boundaries?

_____

_____

16 Why was it so important to the animals to destroy the harness room?

_____

_____

17 What is meant by 'speechless admiration' on line 66?

_____

_____

18–20 The animals' excitement is evident in the final paragraph of this passage. However, the animals will now have a number of issues they need to resolve. List three of them.

_____

_____

_____

_____

_____

_____

20

D 10

Write the **abbreviation** of each of these.

21 please turn over   _____   **22** millilitre   _____

23 France   _____   **24** centigrade   _____

25 Justice of the Peace   _____   **26** identification   _____

27 headquarters   _____   **28** I owe you   _____

8

E 2

Rewrite these **sentences** changing them from **plural** to **singular**.

29–32 The cars skidded as they hit the bollards put out by the policemen to guide the traffic.

_____

_____

33–36 The children sang songs and read stories to the teacher.

_____

_____

8
E 2

Add the **suffix** to each of the words. Rewrite the words correctly.

37 irritate + able _____ **38** transfer + ing _____

39 enter + ance _____ **40** frolic + ing _____

41 necessary + ly _____ **42** defer + ed _____

43 collapse + ible _____ **44** machine + ery _____

8
D 4

Add the missing commas to these **sentences**.

45 The spider pounced on its prey wrapping it quickly in its web.

46 If only Nina were here she'd love to see the ponies perform.

47–48 Oscar had grazed his elbow bruised his shin his trousers were ripped and he was sure he had twisted his ankle.

49–51 The blackbirds perched in a row on the fence their orange beaks flashing gave themselves up to the warmth of the sun.

52–55 When camping there is always so much to do such as collecting wood lighting a fire and tending it before one can begin to think about eating.

11
E 2

Write a **metaphor** about each of the following:

56 the moonlight _____

57 waves _____

58 flowers _____

3
D 5

Write the possessive form of each of these **phrases**, i.e. with an apostrophe.

59 the paws of the lions _____

60 the coat of the lady _____

61 the work of the man _____

62 the books of the library _____

63 the honey of the bees _____

64 the watch of the timekeeper _____

6

Write a **homophone** for each of the words.

65 great _____   **66** freeze _____

67 current _____   **68** sight _____

69 we've _____   **70** principle _____

71 patience _____   **72** lesson _____

List five **diminutives**.

73–77 _____   _____   _____

_____   _____

Copy and punctuate the passage correctly.

78–93 Are you coming in or are you just going to sit there all night Bola queried
I dont think it is safe The sign says not to swim in the river and its very hard to
see overhanging branches and weeds in the dark
Come on youll enjoy it… just for a short time Bola tried to persuade Jason

_____

_____

_____

_____

_____

_____

_____

_____

_____

_____

Write an **adjective** beginning with *b* to go with each word. Don't use a colour adjective.

94 _____ baby **95** _____ knife **96** _____ tree

Answers will vary for questions that require children to answer in their own words. Possible answers to most of these questions are given in *italics*.

Paper 1

1 the forest trees
2 his dog
3–4 *Dodder hated Grum and was angry with him because he had killed his friend Otter.*
5 'and the worn smooth appearance of the steel barrel'
6–7 Dodder was given six oak leaves. He used these to stuff in the muzzle of the gun to cause it to backfire on Grum.
8 striped
9–11 *In the author's style the child needs to fill the gap in time. The story needs to flow descriptively, with reference to the already established characters, their emotions and feelings, e.g. Dodder stood for a moment, making sure the Giant didn't move. Slowly, he turned but the squirrel had scampered away at the noise. The Giant lay still, the smoke from his gun forming a curl above his head. Dodder dropped to the forest floor, and rubbing his hands together, walked home.*
12 because reference is made to his 'master' on line 26
13–14 Grum's eyes are described as 'sharp' giving the impression he has good eyesight.
15 because Grum didn't think there was such a thing as a gnome
16 Dodder describes the gun as 'his club that roars' (line 53).
17 the birds
18–20 *The child's description of Dodder using evidence from the passage to support the answer, e.g. angry, calculating, determined, brave, proud: Dodder is calculating, brave, loyal and confident. Upon learning of the death of his friend Otter, Dodder, showing his loyalty, decides to get revenge. He does this by making a plan to kill the Giant. This plan involves preparation and calculation, as he takes the leaves he will need with him. As he undertakes his plan, Dodder shows his bravery because if his plan failed, the Giant would certainly kill him. Dodder, however, is confident and stands his ground as the Giant tries to fire the gun at him.*
21–22 *telephone, telegraph*
23–24 *submarine, subcontract*
25–26 *confront, construct*
27 *enough*
28 *fought*
29 *borough*
30 *though*
31 *plough*
32 Fran was miserable, she felt <u>at</u> her wits' end.
33 The explorer struggled <u>through</u> the opening.
34 Jake's younger brother went down <u>on</u> all fours when pretending to be a cat.
35 (1) preferment
36 (2) preferential
37 (3) preference
38 (4) preferable
39 (5) prefabricate

40–45 *Sentences completed with two clauses; each clause must have a verb, e.g.* Yousef went *to the library to borrow some books as he planned to spend the afternoon reading.*
46 drama/dramatisation
47 rejection
48 government
49 supplier
50 terror
51 expense/expenditure
52 *as cool as a cucumber*
53 *as light as a feather*
54 *like water off a duck's back*
55 *as dead as a dodo*
56 *as mad as a March hare*
57 *as fit as a fiddle*
58 excep<u>t</u>ion
59 ambi<u>t</u>ion
60 transfu<u>s</u>ion
61 crucifi<u>x</u>ion
62 dissua<u>s</u>ion
63 conve<u>ct</u>ion
64 eleva<u>t</u>ion
65 comple<u>t</u>ion
66 conver<u>s</u>ion
67–79 **T**he icy wind froze **P**etra to the core, the forest giving little protection against the increasing snowfall.
    "**W**e must find shelter soon," she yelled to **T**om, "or we will never make it to morning."
80 adjective
81 adjective
82 noun
83 verb
84 preposition
85 preposition
86 could have
87 shall not
88 will not
89 they will
90–91 (1) *a spider's web* (2) *the World Wide Web*
92–96 *connection, connecting, connectable*
95–97 *sensible, sensitive, nonsense*
98–100 *happiness, happily, unhappy*

Paper 2

1 India
2 Empress of India
3 the animals living in the woods/jungle are active and are moving about
4 mail that is transported over land to be delivered as opposed to being transported by river or sea
5 'The bags on his back and a cloth round his chin'
6 by rail
7–9 *crossing a river, not being able to use the road, climbing a cliff, travelling a long way, carrying heavy mail bags, walking through a storm, climbing up and down steep hills, travelling through different types of land*
10–11 The poem begins in the evening. *This is shown in the lines 'The woods are astir at the close of the day'; 'With a jingle of bells as the dusk gathers in'.*

12–13 The poem ends in the morning. *This is shown in the line 'The world is awake, and the clouds are aglow'.*

14–16 retreat – *back away, run away, withdraw*
ravine – *canyon, gorge, narrow valley*
abode – *home, habitat*

17 *There are no excuses for not delivering the mail.*

18 *'In the Name of the Empress'* or *'While the breath's in his mouth, he must bear without fail'*

19 *It means that the mail carrier is moving quickly.*

20 *The poem is about a mail carrier who doesn't let anything stop him from delivering the mail despite the fact that he has to carry it a long way through difficult circumstances.*

21 She <u>walked</u> slowly to school.

22 For the first time he <u>looked</u> Hannah in the eye.

23–24 The ship <u>sank</u> back down and <u>disappeared</u> forever.

25–27 Niall <u>had come</u> to a halt outside the shop window, but a crowd <u>rushed</u> past and hurried him on.

28–35 *The listed homophones used correctly in the child's own sentence, e.g. We took the dual carriageway to Windsor to watch the men duel. Whose job is it to decide who's sitting where? The council met after lunch to offer counsel. A draft plan was made to block the cold draught.*

36–40 Elizabeth, Victorian, Cardiff, New Guinea, Shakespeare

41–44 *first-born, thirty-five, well-behaved, left-handed*

45 Better late than never.

46 Blood is thicker than water.

47 Every cloud has a silver lining.

48 A penny for your thoughts.

49 More haste, less speed.

50 Many hands make light work.

51 classes   **52** series

53 ellipses   **54** kilos

55 chiefs   **56** cacti

57 trout   **58** elves

59–61 The birds sang in the trees near the fountains.

62–65 They won tickets to watch some local comedians perform.

66–68 The children were splashing the elderly swimmers.

69 *alive, thriving, common*

70 *fluid, melted, boiling*

71 *foe, enemy*

72 *open, unwrap*

73 *vacant, idle*

74 *wide, broad*

75 *study, gaze*

76 *kind, considerate*

77 *decrease, reduce*

78 *underdeveloped, undeveloped*

79–82 Ben asked whether it was time for lunch as he was starving. Tariq suggested they sit on the beach so they could feed the seagulls.

83 (3)   **84** (6)

85 (8)   **86** (7)

87 (4)   **88** (5)

89 (2)   **90** (1)

91 therefore   **92** while

93 as   **94** p<u>ie</u>ce

95 bes<u>ie</u>ge   **96** dec<u>ei</u>t

97 w<u>ei</u>rd   **98** rev<u>ie</u>w

99 exper<u>ie</u>nce   **100** anc<u>ie</u>nt

Paper 3

1 early evening

2 to reassure them that it was he who was coming

3 the gamekeeper

4 *If the boys were to try to catch the pheasants, the pheasants would panic, running in many different directions.*

5–6 *The gamekeeper caught the pheasant by gently moving towards it and then reading what it might do next, getting close enough until he was able to catch it in the net.*

7 to make slight movements, diverting attention

8 *caught, entangled*

9 to restrain the wings so the birds can't fly

10–12 *Ian is the younger of the two boys. This is shown when he keeps pestering his dad even after his dad has explained why he can't help catch the pheasants. It is also shown by his dad's opinion that John would have been able to unfasten the brails, but that Ian would have caused aggravation and taken too long to do so.*

13–16 *The child needs to use evidence from the passage to support his/her comments on the characters of the two boys, e.g. John is a sensible, trustworthy child who is a support to his father. This is shown by his attitude to helping his father and by how well he listens to his father. Ian is more immature and doesn't pay attention when his dad is telling him that he can't do something, so gets in trouble. This is shown when his dad has to tell him not to stick his face down at the pheasants because he will just frighten them.*

17 *The cock hadn't flown for some time and therefore was unsteady in flight, or, it had just been released from a sack which might have confused its senses.*

18 The men were poachers and were preparing to catch the pheasants.

19–20 *The gamekeeper must have felt upset and frustrated as the men were threatening all he works for. He would certainly do something, either approach the men himself, call the police or quietly watch them before scaring them off.*

21 nurs<u>e</u>ry   **22** cam<u>e</u>ra

23 valu<u>a</u>ble   **24** strawberry

25 veg<u>e</u>table   **26** int<u>e</u>rest

27–29 *factory, marmalade, machinery, parliament*

30 There weren't any dolphins swimming by the boat./ There were no dolphins swimming by the boat.

31 Daniel didn't play in the football match.

32 The spelling test wasn't very hard this week.

33 Denholm didn't want a piano lesson.

34 Alex wasn't late for school.

35 Mr Thomas hadn't caught any fish after three hours!

36 wept   **37** threw

38 wrote   **39** was

40 had

41–45 *Five words of common gender, e.g. athlete, friend, headteacher, student, journalist, judge, parent*

46–54 <u>It</u> looked up at <u>them</u> with sad, droopy eyes. How could <u>they</u> consider leaving <u>him</u>? <u>They</u> bundled the shivering dog into the blanket to keep <u>him</u> warm. <u>She</u> wouldn't have to know <u>who</u> had taken <u>him</u>!

55–61 *shan't, wouldn't, I've, would've, won't, haven't, I'll*

62 *Don't tell lies.*

63 *Don't spend all your time worrying about something unimportant.*

64 SW	**65** BEd
66 bros	**67** ROM
68 m²	**69** co.
70 HRH	**71** etc.

72–75 My mum spends hours making all our presents. She makes candlesticks that look like trees, biscuit barrels that look like dog kennels, water-bottle-holders that attach to your arm and many other unusual gifts. Most people love the presents, showing them off to friends and neighbours. However, sometimes you can tell they aren't very pleased!

76 humorous	**77** courageous
78 rebellious	**79** prestigious
80 gaseous	**81** nutritious
82 cautious	**83** gracious

84–91

No. of syllables	Word		
3		*syllable*	*fabulous*
4	*stationary*	*exceptional*	*geography*
5	*sociology*	*electricity*	*organisation*

92–94 *anytime, anywhere, anybody*

95–97 *handshake, handout, underhand*

98–100 *timetable, meantime, overtime*

Paper 4

1 inventor

2 Egyptians

3 by accident when sand was heated with limestone and wood ash

4–5 *over time information has been lost or destroyed; records were never kept initially*

6 *in this case where a particular coin had a particular value for exchange*

7 The clock still works despite its age.

8 *Watches are now a smaller, more manageable size and can be worn on the wrist instead of having to be carried around.*

9 graphite and wood

10 Elizabethan

11 *It comes from a place in France called Nimes, where the material first originated. In French you would say 'de Nimes' meaning 'from Nimes'.*

12–13 An invention chosen by the child and written about in as few words as possible. Compare their answer with the passage to decide how effectively they have achieved this. For example, *World Wide Web, 1989: created by Briton Tim Berners-Lee to transmit information into computers in different parts of the world. Berners-Lee, working in a nuclear research laboratory, wrote the software and then made it freely available.*

14–16 *The invention of the World Wide Web has been important as it has increased the speed of communication, it has allowed easy access to a huge amount of information and has enabled people to do a number of things (e.g. shopping, banking) from their own home.*

17 *He provided his invention free to the world.*

18–20 The child's description of which invention they feel has had the biggest impact on their life and why, e.g. *The World Wide Web has had the biggest impact on my life because I use it every day. It helps me learn about things I would never otherwise know because it would be too hard to find the information. It also lets me interact with other people who live far away. Finally, it means my mum is able to work from home as she uses the web to run her own business.*

21–22 kneeling, run

23–24 two, enthusiastic

25–26 it, they

27–28 with, by

29–51 "Go back to your lesson," said Mrs Patel, "and let me hear no more about it."
"But…" began Sam.
Mrs Patel leaned forward. "I mean it," she said with menace.
"I'll go," Sam replied, and entered the classroom with her head bowed.

52 beneficial	**53** essential
54 influential	**55** superficial
56 initial	**57** prejudicial

58–65

Synonyms	Antonyms
foreseen/expected	fortunate/unlucky
knightly/magnanimous	liberal/conservative
plethora/abundance	appalling/appealing
grand/dignified	demolish/retain

66 lyrics	**67** posterity
68 salad	**69** census
70 nickname	**71** *busily*
72 *hurriedly*	**73** *daintily*
74 *craftily*	**75** *strongly*
76 *carefully*	**77** *accidentally*
78 *loudly*	

79 The ground beneath our feet began to shake, red wheels roared through clouds of steam; they were pulling tanks, guns and ammunition.

80 The question won't be pushed to the back of my mind; on the contrary it fills my every waking moment.

81 The water doesn't run properly, only a trickle; the cupboards are bare, apart from half a packet of stale biscuits.

82 Ling Sung practises his piano very hard; Raj doesn't practise and is still the best!

83 (3)	**84** (5)
85 (4)	**86** (1)
87 (6)	**88** (2)

89–91 *a clause (a section of a sentence with a verb) added to the beginning of each sentence, e.g. causing the girl's umbrella to turn inside out.*

92 *imitating a sound*

93 *another language*

94 *name of a place or person*

95 *preferred*

96 nuisance
97 apparent
98 immediately
99 disastrous
100 conscience

Paper 5

1–2 Mr Jones had lost money in a lawsuit and had started drinking heavily.

3 'Now, as it turned out, the Rebellion was achieved much earlier and more easily than anyone had expected.'

4–5 *They were being neglected and they were not being fed. Mr Jones was not taking care of the farm and it was starting to fall apart.*

6 *with one mind, to be in agreement*

7 the middle of summer

8 *They hadn't been fed all day. They had been beaten.*

9–10 The child's own description of the type of man Mr Jones is, as described in the passage, e.g. *Mr Jones is an unhappy man who no longer takes pride in himself or the farm. He has become lazy, uncaring and is no longer taking good care of the animals or the farm. This is shown when he fails to feed the animals.*

11 four

12–13 An answer demonstrating the child's understanding of how the men would have felt faced with this situation, e.g. *The men were surprised and frightened when the animals turned against them because they only tried to defend themselves for a moment before running away.*

14 a bird

15 *to check that all humans had been chased from the farm*

16 *For the animals the harness room represented the control the humans had had over them.*

17 *The animals were so satisfied and pleased with what they had achieved they could find no words to express themselves.*

18–20 *The animals need to resolve who will now take control of the running of the farm, how they will get the food they need, how they will harvest the hay that is ready to be stored and how they will repair the farm and the fields.*

21 PTO
22 ml
23 Fr
24 C
25 JP
26 ID
27 HQ
28 IOU

29–32 The car skidded as it hit the bollard put out by the policeman to guide the traffic.

33–36 The child sang a song and read a story to the teacher.

37 irritable
38 transferring
39 entrance
40 frolicking
41 necessarily
42 deferred
43 collapsible
44 machinery

45 The spider pounced on its prey, wrapping it quickly in its web.

46 If only Nina were here, she'd love to see the ponies perform.

47–48 Oscar had grazed his elbow, bruised his shin, his trousers were ripped and he was sure he had twisted his ankle.

49–51 The blackbirds, perched in a row on the fence, their orange beaks flashing, gave themselves up to the warmth of the sun.

52–55 When camping, there is always so much to do, such as collecting wood, lighting a fire and tending it, before one can begin to think about eating.

56–58 *a metaphor for each of the given subjects, e.g. the moonlight was a bright ribbon, the waves were lashing the shore, the flowers danced in the breeze*

59 the lions' paws
60 the lady's coat
61 the man's work
62 the library's books
63 the bees' honey
64 the timekeeper's watch
65 grate
66 frieze/frees
67 currant
68 site
69 weave
70 principal
71 patients
72 lessen

73–77 five diminutives (a word that implies smallness) listed, e.g. *booklet, statuette, piglet, duckling, majorette*

78–93 "Are you coming in, or are you just going to sit there all night?" Bola queried.
"I don't think it is safe. The sign says not to swim in the river and it's very hard to see overhanging branches and weeds in the dark."
"Come on you'll enjoy it… just for a short time," Bola tried to persuade Jason.

94 *bouncy*
95 *blunt*
96 *burnt*
97 decompress
98 irretrievable
99 infallible
100 impertinent

Paper 6

1 the 'Big Bang'

2 it fuses to form helium

3 they are rocky planets with metal cores

4–5 'mantle' – *covering*
'coalescing' – *combining*

6–7 *It is possible that there might be life on other planets as gas and water vapour activity, similar to that on Earth, was happening on them as well. However, what these other planets don't have is a similar temperature which allows life to flourish.*

8 Gases released when forming the atmosphere also released water vapour that condensed and formed the oceans.

9 in the oceans

10 *Reference is made to the Goldilocks story in relation to the temperature of the porridge and the 'just right' temperature of Earth, e.g. It is described as the Goldilocks planet because as in the fairy tale in which the temperature of the porridge was just right for Goldilocks, the temperature of Earth is neither too hot nor too cold, but just right to allow life.*

11 When Earth and another planet collided, part of the Earth's crust was thrown off and eventually combined to form the Moon.

12 *Without the Moon living things would not be as they are today, including us.*

13 *Out of all the planets it is only Earth that had the combination of gases and water vapour with the right temperature and the influence of the Moon to create a planet that allows people to live.*

14 because it revolves around Earth

15 profound – *deep, meaningful*

16–17 *The collision broke up the Earth's crust which means the continental plates move around more easily it also tilted the Earth to about 23 degrees off the perpendicular which effects day length and seasonal change.*

18–20 The child's own description of the effect on day length, temperature and animal habits due to the tilt of the Earth, e.g. *If Earth had not been tilted we would have the same length of day everywhere all year, we wouldn't have any seasons and we would have more deserts.*

21 six spiders' webs

22 two girls' dresses

23 Jack's towels

24 four children's food

25 a tulip's petals

26 five steep stairs

27–38 Fran could see **nothing** in the heavy snow that was **settling** around him. He walked forward a couple more **paces** but panic gripped him, he felt so alone and **isolated**, if only he had **heeded** his father's warning. Quickly he rushed back to the **protection** of the fallen, **hollow** tree. At least there he would be able to protect himself from the **shroud** of snow and **biting** winds. He cuddled himself, sobbing **inwardly**, his hands already **numb** with the cold. **Someone** was sure to find him soon... he hoped.

39–42 *The four sentences, each with a modal verb included, e.g. The dog would often sleep in the sun. Eleni will talk to her teacher after the lesson. Tyler could do his homework at my house. The workmen might work through the night.*

43–46 Please provide the goats, morning and evening with: fresh water, available hay, a scoop of concentrates and milk for the kids.

47–48 Please bring the following to school on Monday: swimming costume, towel and bag.

49–50 In the afternoon Daniel arrived in Cambridge, drew up his cart in the market place, unloaded his wares and began to draw a crowd.

51 Gaby heard Sally's voice replying; she sounded terrified.

52–54 A thrush appeared from under a bush by the lawn, nervously jumping, pecking, listening to the sounds around.

55 half
56 canoe
57 hoof
58 index
59 waif
60 radio
61 stimulus
62 crisis

63 (1) proper noun/noun
64 (2) verb
65 (3) definite article
66 (4) preposition
67 (5) adverb
68 (6) pronoun
69 (7) preposition
70 (8) pronoun
71 *forest*
72 *number*
73 *demand*
74 *perfection*
75 *uneasy*
76 *award*

77 The hot air balloon bounced <u>when</u> it landed in the field.

78 Let's sit by the playground <u>so</u> we can see the children playing.

79 Class 5's assembly was very funny <u>because</u> Toby tripped off the stage!

80 The storm brought 90 mph winds <u>and</u> snow drifted, causing traffic chaos.

81 Gradually the days became shorter <u>as</u> winter approached.

82–89 producer, conductor, teacher, giant, actor, builder, audience, nurse

90 parliament
91 imaginary
92 complimentary
93 desperately
94 conscientious
95 sincerely
96 privilege
97 marvellous
98 *Manchester, England, Bath Rugby Club*
99 *love, hate, guilt*
100 *swarm, herd, orchestra, pride, gaggle*

Paper 7

1 rainy

2 *'Reading between the lines' is when a person doesn't look just at the words being written or said, but rather tries to figure out what the author/speaker is really trying to express.*

3–4 *bullets and shells raining down; the bright lights and glow of the sky when the bombs and gunfire go off*

5 The mother was concerned that her son wasn't telling her what was really going on and that he might be in danger.

6 He was trying to protect them from the horrors of the war.

7–8 *The young man would have felt confused as they had encouraged him to give the details, and hurt as he felt a lack of support for the reality of the situation.*

9 it is about people after the war has ended

10 *It means that people should promise on the lives of the men who were killed that they will never forget the horrors of the war.*

11 *to show people the horrors of war; the horrors the soldiers had to suffer*

12 *The lines are about a man who feels angry and sorry for his exhausted men who have to continue fighting a war.*

13 *The faces of the young soldiers who, when the war began, were happy and optimistic are now tired and troubled.*

14–15 *The poet is trying to make sure that now that the war is over, people remember what it was like and the sacrifices made by those who died. He wants*

Bond English Assessment Papers 11⁺–12⁺ years Book 2

people to remember the horror of war so they don't rush into another one. One way this is shown is by his repetition of the phrase 'Have you forgotten yet?' which, by being repeated, makes the reader really think about what it means.

16–18 *The child's own summary of how these two poems make them feel and why, using evidence from each poem, e.g. The two poems make me feel sad and angry. I feel sad because the poems show the effect of war on young men and the terrible things they must see and do. In the first poem, the young man tries to share with his parents what is happening to him but they don't want to know about it because it is so awful. This means that he can't talk to them about it which is sad. The second poem shows the terrible situations the soldiers are in with the rats and how they started out happy but as a result of being in the war have become upset and sad.*

19–20 *The child's own response indicating an understanding that the use of graphic details and images allows the reader to have a real sense of what war is actually like. The response should also indicate the child's opinion on whether the poems would be less or more effective without this sort of language, but the response must be fully explained, e.g. The poets used the disturbing details because war is so horrible and they wanted to make sure the reader had a sense of what it was actually like. I believe that without these sorts of detail it would be hard for people who have never been in a war to understand exactly what it is like and they might have a false impression that war isn't so bad.*

21	active	**22**	active
23	passive	**24**	passive
25	active	**26**	passive

27–29 Three conditional sentences, where one thing depends on something else, e.g. *Gran will take the cake out of the oven because I have to go to work.*

30	certain	**31**	here
32	you	**33**	book
34	gave	**35**	will
36	spoke	**37**	said
38	station@ry	**39**	sep@rate
40	int@rest	**41**	math@matics
42	ordin@ry	**43**	fatt@ning

44–46 Three words of the child's choice with unstressed vowels.

47 The <u>weather-beaten, broken</u> door swung in the wind.

48 As the sun began to set, the mildew settled on the <u>short and stubbly</u> grass.

49 Mum served the <u>thick, lumpy pile</u> of porridge for breakfast.

50–51 Two sentences written by the child, each with an adjectival phrase.

52–65 "Andrea, for goodness sake, hurry up!"
Her father's voice, curt with frustration, sounded all the way up to her bedroom.
"Andrea! Come down this minute!"

66–67 *whoosh, swish*
68–69 *trickle, splash*
70–71 *slam, squeak*

72	avoidable	**73**	appreciable
74	collapsible	**75**	debatable

76	responsible	**77**	believable
78	regrettable	**79**	intelligible
80	*across*	**81**	*underneath*
82–83	*Below, through*	**84**	*in*
85	*over*	**86**	made
87	understood	**88**	thought
89	threw	**90**	was
91	went		

92 *snow covered the field so it was all you could see*
93 *the sky red from the setting sun*
94 *an owl flew as the wind whipped through trees making a spooky sound*

95	lazy	**96**	tidy
97	contribute	**98**	direct
99	merge	**100**	accuse

Paper 8

1 BBC World Service Trust
2 radios playing martial music
3 A survey was carried out on Africa's many different types of media.

4–5 The governments in Africa generally are strong. This is shown by the control they have over the media; for example, by not advertising with a television station, they can cause it to fail as it won't have many other ways of getting money.

6–8 stymied – *having its activities blocked*
fosters – *promotes the growth and development of something*
conventional – *doing things according to tradition*

9 *Being an independent charity means that the organisation doesn't have any ulterior motive for writing the report and that its findings are not biased or created so that it would benefit in some way, such as by making money.*

10 *The state broadcasters only say what the government tells them to say. They put forward only the government's point of view.*

11–12 *The report suggests that if the media were able to have freedom it would be to the benefit of the people who live in the country; they would be able to make their own decisions based on the facts rather than what the governments choose for them to know.*

13 It is controlled by the government and therefore they decide what is to be printed

14 *'Freedom of information' is important because it allows ordinary citizens to learn what their government is doing and to have access to information they need.*

15 seventeen
16 *growing quickly*

17 *They might want information about the candidates or laws they support to become known and possibly chosen because these candidates or laws might benefit their own business or beliefs.*

18–20 The child's own view of how things might change in this country if our media were denied their freedom to report things, e.g. *fewer reins on government, more corruption, less accountability of politicians, police, industrial leaders, etc.*

21 can
22 should

A6

23 could   24 must

25 *musicians*   26 *dancers*

27 *lions*   28 aperitifs

29 funguses or fungi   30 crises

31 memos   32 wharfs or wharves

33 salmon   34 lice

35 methodologies

36–37 (self-centred) gratifying <u>unselfish</u> respectable

38–39 goodness debate (unjust) <u>fairness</u>

40–41 generate <u>purify</u> (grubby) mean

42–43 <u>emaciated</u> elevate beneath (stunning)

44–45 search <u>reveal</u> misrepresent (hide)

46–48 Rupa's face looked dreadful, red and swollen, she was gasping for breath; but selfish Karen did not care.

49–50 As Tim was winched up, the shock of nearly being devoured by the lions hit him; his whole body began to shake.

51–52 We'd had a fabulous holiday touring Thailand, Cambodia and Singapore; then the tsunami struck.

53–55 *insurance, abundance, resistance*

56–58 *contagious, dangerous, marvellous*

59–61 *considerable, adorable, tolerable*

62 has   63 are

64 thought   65 swam

66 threw   67 is

68 deport   69 disagree

70 dangle   71 data

72 drizzle   73 discuss

74 dreary   75 dubious

76–91 **M**r **D**avey owned the small, well-stocked sweet shop in **P**ortscatho. **E**ach summer holiday we would rush down the cobbled streets, fighting to get there first. "**M**orning boys," he'd mutter, as we clambered to choose our sweets.

92 verb   93 noun

94 adjective   95 adverb

96 condemn   97 psychology

98 mortgage   99 guarantee

100 gourmet

Paper 9

1 Denis

2 a wrestler

3 importunes access to you

4–5 to find out news at the court; to discover the fate of Rosalind; to learn where the old Duke is living

6 they are brothers

7 her cousin, the new Duke's daughter, is fond of her and arranged for her to stay

8 The lords weren't stopped as the new duke gained their land and income.

9 Reference is made to Robin Hood as the old Duke has taken cover in woods and has a band of followers much as Robin Hood did.

10 flock to – *rush to, gather in groups to go and see*

11 As this is a play, the information in italics gives directions so the actors and people reading the play know what actions are being taken.

12 Rosalind is troubled because her father has been banished.

13 cousin

14 mirth – *happiness, joy*

15 Celia maintains that had the roles been reversed she would have taken Rosalind's father as her own.

16 Celia promises Rosalind will inherit what she would have had previously.

17 She means that something bad should happen to her if she breaks her promise to Rosalind.

18–19 *a rose is a beautiful object; it is a play on her name which has the sound 'rose' in it*

20 Rosalind promises that she will forget about her problems and be pleased for Celia.

21 the farmer's chicken coop

22 the six ducks' eggs

23 the last fledgling's mother

24 the twelve lions' cubs

25 the old pony's reins

26 the three cats' muddy paws

27 (3)   28 (5)

29 (7)   30 (1)

31 (4)   32 (8)

33 (6)   34 (2)

35 passive   36 active

37 passive   38 passive

39 active   40 active

41 *to make a fresh start*

42 *something good always comes out of something bad*

43 *not to take sides*

44 *people who don't waste things are less likely to be short of important things*

45 *a complete surprise*

46 *to say things as you see them*

47–50 The child should make up their own mnemonic, a way to remember a particular spelling, for each of the four words listed, e.g. **s**ome **e**nglish **p**ears **a**nd **r**aisins **a**re **t**erribly **e**njoyable or <u>a rat</u> can be found in sep<u>arat</u>e.

51 *where, when, because, as*

52 *or*

53 *once, when, after*

54 *while*

55–62 The words in bold used in both a statement (a formal account of facts) and then a question, e.g. Statement: *During bad weather it is important to watch for fallen trees in the road.* Question: *Have you heard whether the bad weather has caused a tree to fall in the road?*

63 *mouse*   64 *ox*

65 *moon/grave*   66 *ice*

67 *star/button*   68 *nails*

69 gover**n**ment   70 liaison

71 February   72 acco**mm**odation

73 tranquillity   74 super**s**ede

75 conven**ie**nce   76 advertis**e**ment

77 i**mm**inent   78 extrava**g**ant

79–84 They walked home again, there being nothing more of interest to see. As they came in through the front-door of the big house, the first thing Tom heard was the ticking of the grandfather clock. It would tick on to bedtime, and in that way Time was Tom's friend; but, after that, it would tick on to Saturday, and in that way Time was Tom's enemy.

Bond English Assessment Papers 11+–12+ years Book 2

85 humorous   86 hungry
87 disastrous   88 reliable
89 *The lesson is about to begin.*
90 *I will try to do my best.*
91 *Why don't you leave early?*
92 *Shall I come to your house or would you like to come to mine?*
93–94 hex = six, *hexagon*
95–96 circum = around, *circumference*
97–98 micro = small, *microscope*
99–100 il = not, *illegal*

Paper 10

1 He was feeling a little restless and needed to go exploring/Because George Orwell is buried there.
2 because it has two names, Chilswell Valley or Happy Valley
3 The Thames
4 American
5–6 The British Isles, called 'little' because compared to America they are small.
7 *two men who are famous across the world*
8 yes
9 his name is actually Eric Arthur Blair
10 Asquith's inscription states that he was Prime Minister of England whereas in fact he was Prime Minister of Great Britain.
11–13 impetuously – *acting on impulse*
terse – *concise, curt*
anonymous – *unknown*
14–15 *According to Bill, Iowa didn't have many famous people buried there as he states, 'We in Iowa would be proud of either of them – indeed we would be proud of Trigger the Wonder Horse or the guy who invented traffic cones or pretty much anyone at all.'*
16–17 The child highlighting two amusing sentences/ happenings in the passage, e.g. *the currant bun feet and his statement about Asquith's descendants.*
18–20 The child's e-mail responding to the query about Sutton Courtenay. It should include the overall impression that Bill gives of his visit to Sutton Courtenay in the passage and reflect his thoughts on whether it was worthwhile going. It should also be in the same tone or style as the rest of the passage, e.g. *Cheers, from this side of the pond. Yes, indeed, Sutton Courtenay is well worth a visit, but beware of the mud if you plan on coming during the rainy season. There are three lovely pubs that would make a good stopping place before you visit the graves at the church. It might be worth taking biographies of both Orwell and Asquith as you might not recognise them from their headstones. Wishing you all the best on your adventure, Bill.*
21–22 movie, *baseball*
23–24 encore, *restaurant*
25–26 spaghetti, *piano*

27–28 pyjamas, *curry*
29 best   30 longest
31 Most   32 tastiest
33 most wonderful   34 least
35 worst
36–40 Six sentences with an adjectival phrase (a group of words describing a noun) added to improve each one, e.g. *Mr Trump, the grouchy old man that he was, chased the children out of his garden.*
41 advertiser   42 musician
43 absentee   44 admirer
45 assistant   46 cashier
47 imitator   48 magician
49 teacher   50 competitor
51 *pop*   52 *bang*
53 *tick*   54 *plop*
55 *slap*   56 *tinkle*
57 *e.g. I bought a hand-made card for my sister.*
58 *Tuhil won the long-distance road race.*
59 *e.g. Mia swam the 100m in a record-breaking time.*
60 *e.g. Dad couldn't find his short-sleeved shirt.*
61 *stealthily, sneakily*
62 *politely, respectfully*
63 *frequently, loudly*
64 *breathlessly, excitedly*
65–72 A short argument including the words/phrases in bold, about whether boxing should be banned. Each word/phrase needs to be used in its correct context, e.g. *It is my **opinion** that boxing should be banned because I **believe** that it is a dangerous activity. **Although** others may have a different **viewpoint**, it is my **contention** that because so many people who box have health problems, it should be stopped right away. **Furthermore**, it is my **conclusion** that boxing should be banned in England **as well as** the rest of Europe.*
73 *depression, impression*
74 *unhappily, unhappiness*
75 *unlocked*
76 *disagreeable, disagreement*
77 *returnable*
78 *mistaken*
79 *co-operation, co-operated*
80 *undoing*
81–100 As Monty raced off down the beach, Brian and Jess began to feel a little concerned. Monty was a lovely black Labrador who was a little unreliable when it came to listening to commands. "Monty, come back!" called Jess. "We've got to go home." But Monty seemed not to hear. He put his nose down to the sand, picked up a scent of something good and was off.
"You'd better wait here, I'll chase after him," suggested Brian, beginning to feel annoyed with his disobedient dog.

Add a **prefix** to make each of these words into its **antonym**.

97 compress _____ **98** retrievable _____

99 fallible _____ **100** pertinent _____

Now go to the Progress Chart to record your score!   Total   100

Paper 6

The Lucky Planet

Our solar system was created between 4.5 and 5 billion years ago. The Sun and
planets were formed from a huge cloud of dust and gas produced in the Big Bang.
Gravity caused the cloud to collapse towards its centre and begin to rotate. At the
centre of this spinning disc, temperatures rose to a point where hydrogen fused to
form helium and our Sun was born. Further out, dust particles were drawn together   5
by electrostatic and other forces and gradually grew into larger and larger rocks.
Gravity drew these rocks together, and slowly these bodies grew to form the planets.
The four planets nearest the Sun – Mercury, Venus, Earth and Mars – were made
up largely of solid material with high melting points, rocky planets with metal cores.
Further away from the Sun are the gas giants – Jupiter, Saturn, Uranus and Neptune.   10

Early in its history, our planet began to sort itself into a number of different layers. The natural decay of radioactive material at its centre generated enormous quantities of heat, which melted most of the rock, forming a liquid 'mantle'. Around this mantle – and no thicker, relatively, than the skin on a peach – formed the cooler solid crust. Then, as still today, the molten rock regularly erupted through the thin surface layer. This volcanic activity was accompanied by the release of gases such as nitrogen and carbon dioxide that formed the basis of our planet's atmosphere. With the gases came water vapour in such large quantities that when it condensed it formed the oceans, and it was in those oceans that the first simple life forms evolved 4 billion years ago.

Volcanic activity and the release of gases and water vapour were also happening on Earth's near neighbours, but as far as we know, no life has evolved on any other planets in our solar system. The main reason for this seems to be simple cosmic luck… Our planet, though – orbiting at 149.6 million km (93 million miles) from the Sun – seems to be at just the right distance for life. Our medium-thick atmosphere has contained just the right amount of carbon dioxide to help keep Earth at a perfect average surface temperature of 17°C (63°F). We live on the 'Goldilocks' planet because, just like the porridge in the fairy tale, Earth is neither too hot nor too cold but 'just right' for life.

Looking back to Earth from the Moon, the astronauts may not have fully realised the vital role the satellite they were standing on has played, and still plays, in creating and maintaining life on Earth. It has been the architect of evolution, and without it, we probably would not be here today. Again, cosmic luck was on our side. It is generally believed that the Moon was formed about 4.5 billion years ago, when a planet about the size of Mars collided with the early Earth. The huge impact threw into space an enormous quantity of the Earth's crust, which orbited the planet before gradually coalescing to form the Moon…

The impact was to have profound influences. So much of the Earth's surface was thrown into space to form the Moon that only about 30 per cent of the original crust was left. What remained was so thin that the continental plates moved around more easily. This continental drift has played a key role in driving evolution… In the process, new and different habitats have constantly been created, and a wide variety of life evolved to exploit these new and changing environments. Without the collision that created the Moon, the plates would be locked together as they are on Venus, and there would be far fewer habitats on Earth today.

The collision had one other dramatic effect. It knocked our planet so that it was no longer spinning on a straight axis with respect to the Sun. The angle of the tilt it created was roughly 23 degrees off the perpendicular, and that tilt remains today. Without this, life on Planet Earth would be very different. Day length all over the world would be the same all year round. The Sun's warming influence would also remain constant throughout the year and there would be no seasonal change. Without the warmth of summer, the poles would on average be far colder, and their frozen influence would extend further towards the equator. There would be no cycle of wet and dry seasons in the subtropical regions, and the world's deserts would be far more extensive. There would be no need for animals to migrate, and life would probably be far less diverse.

15

20

25

30

35

40

45

50

55

From *Planet Earth* by Alistair Fothergill

Answer these questions.

1 What caused our solar system to form? _____

2 What happens to hydrogen in extremely high temperatures?

_____

3 What do the four nearest planets to the Sun have in common?

_____

_____

4–5 What is the meaning of the following words?

mantle (line 13): _____

coalescing (line 37): _____

6–7 Using evidence from the passage, give one argument for and one argument against the possibility of life on other planets.

_____

_____

_____

_____

8 In your own words describe how the oceans were formed.

_____

_____

_____

9 Where on Earth did the first life forms evolve? _____

10 Describe in your own words why Earth is described as the 'Goldilocks' planet.

_____

_____

11 How was the Moon formed? _____

_____

_____

12 Why is the Moon described as 'the architect of evolution' (line 32)?

_____

_____

_____

13 Why is this passage entitled 'The Lucky Planet'?

_____

_____

_____

_____

14 Why is the Moon described as being Earth's satellite (line 31)?

_____

15 Write a synonym for 'profound' (line 38). _____

16–17 Name two ways the collision Earth suffered make it the planet it is today.

_____

_____

_____

_____

18–20 In your own words, describe three characteristics of what our planet would be like had it not been tilted.

_____

_____

_____

_____

_____

_____

◯ 20

D 5

Copy and add any missing apostrophes.

21 six spiders webs _____

22 two girls dresses _____

23 Jacks towels _____

24 four childrens food _____

25 a tulips petals _____

26 five steep stairs _____ ◯ 6

In the following passage there are blanks. The jumbled words in brackets, when the letters are rearranged, make a word to fill each blank. E 2

27–38 Fran could see _____ (innohgt) in the heavy snow that was

_____ (snetitlg) around him. He walked forward a couple more

_____ (ascep) but panic gripped him, he felt so alone and

_____ (istlaode), if only he had _____ (eeeddh) his

father's warning. Quickly he rushed back to the _____ (tprnotecio)

of the fallen, _____ (hllowo) tree. At least there he would be able to

protect himself from the _____ (sorudh) of snow and

_____ (giitnb) winds. He cuddled himself, sobbing

_____ (wyinardl), his hands already _____ (bunm) with

the cold. _____ (Soomeen) was sure to find him soon… he hoped. ◯ 12

Change these **sentences** so they each include a **modal verb**.

39 The dog slept in the sun.

_____

_____

40 Eleni talked to her teacher.

_____

_____

41 Tyler did his homework.

_____

_____

42 The workmen worked through the night.

_____

_____ ◯ 4

Add the missing semi-colons, colons and commas.

43–46 Please provide the goats morning and evening with fresh water available hay a scoop of concentrates and milk for the kids.

47–48 Please bring the following to school on Monday swimming costume towel and bag.

49–50 In the afternoon Daniel arrived in Cambridge drew up his cart in the market place unloaded his wares and began to draw a crowd.

51 Gaby heard Sally's voice replying she sounded terrified.

52–54 A thrush appeared from under a bush by the lawn nervously jumping pecking listening to the sounds around.

12

Write these words in their **singular** form.

E 2

55 halves	_____	**56** canoes	_____
57 hooves	_____	**58** indices	_____
59 waifs	_____	**60** radios	_____
61 stimuli	_____	**62** crises	_____

8

What part of speech is each word in bold?

D 6

    (1)   (2)   (3)   (4)   (5)
Meena thought of **the** dozens **of** beggars who had tried **desperately** to

        (6)   (7) (8)
persuade **them** to part **with their** money.

63 (1) _____	**64** (2) _____	
65 (3) _____	**66** (4) _____	
67 (5) _____	**68** (6) _____	
69 (7) _____	**70** (8) _____	

8

Write a word that falls alphabetically between those listed.

E 2

71 foresight   _____   foretell

72 nugget   _____   numeral

73 delusion   _____   democracy

74 percussion _____ performance

75 unearth _____ unexpected

76 await _____ awkward

Underline the **conjunction** in each of these sentences.

77 The hot air balloon bounced when it landed in the field.

78 Let's sit by the playground so we can see the children playing.

79 Class 5's assembly was very funny because Toby tripped off the stage!

80 The storm brought 90 mph winds and snow drifted, causing traffic chaos.

81 Gradually the days became shorter as winter approached.

Underline the words below that can be used for either gender.

82–89 producer   conductor   duke   teacher

       giant   actor   builder   cockerel

       audience   bull   nurse

Each of these words has a missing letter. Rewrite them correctly.

90 parliment _____   **91** imagnary _____

92 complimentry _____   **93** despertely _____

94 conscientous _____   **95** sincerly _____

96 privilge _____   **97** marvelous _____

List three examples of each type of **noun**.

98 proper noun _____ _____ _____

99 abstract noun _____ _____ _____

100 collective noun _____ _____ _____

6

D 6

5

D 8

8

E 2

8

D 6

3

Paper 7

These poems tell of two soldiers' experiences of war.

APO 96225 was written about the jungle warfare in Vietnam.

A young man once went off to war
in a far country.
When he had time, he wrote home and
said, 'Sure rains here a lot.'

But his mother, reading between the lines,   5
wrote, 'We're quite concerned. Tell us
what it's really like.'

And the young man responded, 'Wow, you ought
to see the funny monkeys!'

To which the mother replied, 'Don't   10
hold back, how is it?'

And the young man wrote, 'The sunsets here
are spectacular.'

In her next letter the mother
wrote, 'Son, we want you to tell us   15
everything.'

So the next time he wrote,
'Today I killed a man.
Yesterday I helped drop napalm on women and
children. Tomorrow we are going to use gas.'   20

And the father wrote, 'Please don't
write such depressing letters. You're upsetting
your mother.'

So, after a while, the young man wrote, 'Sure rains a
lot here...'   25

by Larry Rottman

Answer these questions.

1 What does the young soldier say the weather is like where he is fighting the war?

_____

2 What is meant by 'reading between the lines' (line 5)?

_____

3–4 'Sure rains here a lot' and 'the sunsets here are spectacular' could be
metaphors. To what might the poet have been referring in a war poem?

_____

5 Why was the soldier's mother concerned?

_____

_____

6 Why did the young man not give his parents details of the war initially in his letters?

_____

_____

7–8 How do you think the young man felt on receiving his father's letter? Explain why.

_____

_____

8

B

This poem was written about World War I.

Aftermath
HAVE you forgotten yet?...
For the world's events have rumbled on since those gagged days,
Like traffic checked while at the crossing of city-ways:
And the haunted gap in your mind has filled with thoughts that flow
Like clouds in the lit heaven of life; and you're a man reprieved to go,   5
Taking your peaceful share of Time, with joy to spare.
But the past is just the same – and War's a bloody game...
Have you forgotten yet?...
Look down, and swear by the slain of the War that you'll never forget.

Do you remember the dark months you held the sector at Mametz –   10
The nights you watched and wired and dug and piled sandbags on parapets?
Do you remember the rats; and the stench
Of corpses rotting in front of the front-line trench –
And dawn coming, dirty-white, and chill with a hopeless rain?
Do you ever stop and ask, 'Is it all going to happen again?'   15

Do you remember that hour of din before the attack –
And the anger, the blind compassion that seized and shook you then
As you peered at the doomed and haggard faces of your men?
Do you remember the stretcher-cases lurching back
With dying eyes and lolling heads – those ashen-grey   20
Masks of the lads who once were keen and kind and gay?

Have you forgotten yet?...
Look up, and swear by the green of the spring that you'll never forget.

by Siegfried Sassoon

Answer these questions.

9 Why is the poem called *Aftermath*?

_____

10 Explain the **phrase** 'and swear by the slain of the War that you'll never forget' (line 9).

_____

_____

11 What is the purpose of the information presented in lines 10–14?

_____

_____

12 Look at lines 17–18. Explain what these lines are about.

_____

_____

13 Describe in your own words the lines 'those ashen-grey masks of the lads who once were keen and kind and gay' (lines 20–21).

_____

_____

_____

14–15 In your own words, using evidence from the poem, describe the message the poet is trying to portray.

_____

_____

_____

_____

7

About both poems:

16–18 On reading the two poems, how do they make you feel? Why? Use one line or image from each poem to support your answer.

_____

_____

_____

_____

_____

19–20 Both poems contain graphic and disturbing images and details. Explain why the information the poets wanted to present was so strongly stated. Do you think the poems would be as effective if fewer graphic details were used?

_____

_____

_____

_____

◯ **5**

📖 D 6

State whether each of these **sentences** is **active** or **passive**.

21 Danny ran to school because he was late. _____

22 The dog licked her bone. _____

23 The leaves were cleared up by the caretaker. _____

24 The cake for Holly's party was made by Aunty Sam. _____

25 Kyle tripped at the playground. _____

26 Jade's drink was knocked over by Lisa. _____

◯ **6**

📖 D 2

Complete each of these as **conditional sentences**.

27 Gran will take the cake out of the oven _____.

28 We will go by train _____.

29 Meena might be late home from school _____

_____.

◯ **3**

Write the modern version of each of the following words.

E 2

30 sarten	_____	**31** hither	_____
32 thou	_____	**33** booke	_____
34 gavest	_____	**35** wilt	_____
36 spake	_____	**37** saith	_____

8

E 2

Circle the unstressed vowels.

38 s t a t i o n a r y   **39** s e p a r a t e   **40** i n t e r e s t

41 m a t h e m a t i c s   **42** o r d i n a r y   **43** f a t t e n i n g

44–46 Write down three other words with unstressed vowels.

_____   _____   _____

9

D 2

Underline the **adjectival phrase** in each **sentence**.

47 The weather-beaten, broken door swung in the wind.

48 As the sun began to set, the mildew settled on the short and stubbly grass.

49 Mum served a thick, lumpy pile of porridge for breakfast.

50–51 Write two **sentences**, each with an **adjectival phrase**.

_____

_____

5

D 5

Copy and punctuate this passage correctly.

52–65 andrea for goodness sake hurry up Her father's voice curt with frustration sounded all the way up to her bedroom andrea Come down this minute

_____

_____

_____

_____

_____

_____

14

Write two **onomatopoeic** words associated with each of the following.

C 4

66–67 the wind _____   _____

68–69 a river _____   _____

70–71 a door _____   _____

6

Add the **suffix** *able* or *ible* to the words. Rewrite the words correctly.

E 2

72 avoid _____   **73** appreciate _____

74 collapse _____   **75** debate _____

76 response _____   **77** believe _____

78 regret _____   **79** intelligent _____

8

Complete the following **sentences** by writing a different **preposition** in each space.

D 6

80 The hunters made their way silently _____ the river.

81 The terrified cat hid _____ the bush, just out of reach of the dog.

82–83 _____ the surface of the water, the fish darted _____ the seaweed.

84 To keep the chickens safe they were closed _____ each night.

85 Danielle corresponds with her friends _____ the internet.

6

Write the simple **past tense** of these **verbs**.

D 6

86 to make _____

87 to understand _____

88 to think _____

89 to throw _____

90 to be _____

91 to go _____

6

Explain what each of these **metaphors** means.

92 A blanket of snow covered the fields.

_____

93 the fiery evening sky

_____

94 The owl flew in the haunting wind.

_____

3

Write the **root word** of each of these words.

95 laziness _____

96 tidily _____

97 contributory _____

98 redirected _____

99 submerged _____

100 accusation _____

6

Now go to the Progress Chart to record your score!   Total   100

B

When government holds all the cards

A media boom across Africa is being stymied by tighter government controls, according to a report by the BBC World Service Trust.

Waking up to hear martial music on the radio is said to be the first sign of a coup, but for Africa's press and broadcasters, military takeovers may only be the most extreme example of governments' attempts to tame them.   5

On the face of it, the continent's media are booming. Commercial and community radio is taking off, religious broadcasting is thriving, and there is a new-found taste for tabloid newspapers. But a survey of the continent's media landscape shows that press and broadcasters face an uphill struggle in challenging state power.

The survey by the BBC World Service Trust, an independent charity that fosters   10
the media in developing countries, shows that when governments are powerful and the private sector is weak, the media struggle.

Government often holds all the cards – in many African countries, it is the main advertiser, while state broadcasters act as the voice of the government. In many cases, state broadcasters are also allowed to carry advertising, starving commercial   15
radio and TV of revenue.

Digging a well or buying a Christmas goat are more conventional ways of lifting Africa out of poverty, but liberating the media may be just as crucial to development, the report's backers suggest.

Stephen King, director of the World Service Trust, says: "It's important both in   20
holding governments to account and helping ordinary people to ask politicians questions, things we take for granted in more free media environments."
Constraints on the media can be simple matters of infrastructure. "The only printing press in Ethiopia is owned by the government," says King. "If somebody is printing a newspaper critical of the government, and there are riots on the street, they'll   25
suddenly, mysteriously, find the printing press is locked overnight."

Many African countries lack laws that guarantee freedom of information. In some cases, the laws exist but have yet to be enabled; in two countries, Ghana and Nigeria, such legislation has been pending government approval for up to six years.

Written in collaboration with two African universities and researchers across   30
17 countries, the report paints a picture of a rapidly mushrooming industry.

In the Congo, where elections took place last year, the number of local radio stations increased from eight to 150. There are regular media blips in African countries around election times, reflecting the desire of local businessmen to gain a temporary mouthpiece…   35

The growth often occurs in urban centres where advertisers can target the middle classes. It can be an uncertain business, however – a scarcity of audience research makes many advertisers hesitant to invest. Donors could help set up an audience research bureau, King suggests. The media boom is good for jobs, and plenty of journalists have been hired, but many of them lack qualifications and technical   40
skills. Journalists tend to be poorly paid, the report found. This was especially the case for print journalists. In Nigeria, print reporters often went unpaid for months.

by Jeevan Vasagar

Answer these questions.

1 Which organisation wrote the report? _____

2 What usually is the first sign of a military takeover?

_____

3 A survey has been carried out on Africa's 'media landscape' (line 8). What is meant by this **phrase**?

_____

_____

4–5 Generally, are the governments in Africa deemed to be strong or weak? Use one piece of evidence from the passage to support your answer.

_____

6–8 Give the meaning of the following words as they are used in the passage:

'stymied' (line 1) _____

'fosters' (line 10) _____

'conventional' (line 17) _____

9 Why is it beneficial that the organisation that wrote the report is 'an independent charity' (line 10)?

_____

_____

10 In your own words, explain the **phrase** 'state broadcasters act as the voice of the government'.

_____

_____

11–12 Why do you think the report suggests that 'liberating the media may be... crucial to development'? Use evidence from the passage to support your answer.

_____

_____

_____

_____

_____

13 Why is it a problem that Ethiopia has only one printing press?

_____

_____

14 Why is it important for a country to have 'freedom of information' (line 27)?

_____

_____

_____

15 How many countries were involved with the writing of the report? _____

16 What is meant by the **phrase** 'rapidly mushrooming' (line 31)?

_____

17 Why do you think local businessmen want to have a voice around election times?

_____

_____

_____

_____

18–20 If the government controlled the media in this country, describe three ways you think things might change.

_____

_____

_____

_____

_____

20

Underline the **modal verbs** in each of these sentences.

D 6

21 He can speak Chinese as well as German.

22 You should wear the blue hat.

23 We could try to fix your bike.

24 I must go now.

4

Write what these **collective nouns** are used to describe.

D 6

25 a band   _____

26 a company   _____

27 a pride   _____

3

Write the **plural** form of each of these words.

E 2

28 aperitif	_____	29 fungus	_____
30 crisis	_____	31 memo	_____
32 wharf	_____	33 salmon	_____
34 louse	_____	35 methodology	_____

8

Underline the word on each line which is a **synonym** of the word in bold, and ring the word which is its **antonym**.

D 9

36–37 **selfless**	self-centred	gratifying	unselfish	respectable
38–39 **justice**	goodness	debate	unjust	fairness
40–41 **clean**	generate	purify	grubby	mean
42–43 **haggard**	emaciated	elevate	beneath	stunning
44–45 **disclosure**	search	reveal	misrepresent	hide

10

Add the missing semicolons and commas to these **sentences**.

D 4
D 5

46–48 Rupa's face looked dreadful red and swollen she was gasping for breath but selfish Karen did not care.

49–50 As Tim was winched up the shock of nearly being devoured by the lions hit him his whole body began to shake.

51–52 We'd had a fabulous holiday touring Thailand Cambodia and Singapore then the tsunami struck.

7

Write three words using each of these **suffixes**.

E 2

53–55 ance _____ _____ _____

56–58 ous _____ _____ _____

59–61 able _____ _____ _____

○ 9

Underline the correct word in the brackets.

D 6

62 Jess (have, has) forgotten her glasses again!

63 When (is, are) you going to tidy your room?

64 I (think, thought) it was time to do my homework.

65 They (swim, swam) 1 km to raise money for the homeless.

66 Raj (threw, throw) the ball for his dog.

67 When (is, are) Kate arriving?

○ 6

Write a word, beginning with *d*, which has the same meaning as the word on the left.

D 9

68 remove   de_____

69 to conflict   di_____

70 hang   da_____

71 information   da_____

72 rain   dr_____

73 to talk   di_____

74 dull   dr_____

75 doubtful   du_____

○ 8

Rewrite the passage, separating the words correctly and adding the missing capital letters and punctuation.

D 4
D 5

76–91 mrdaveyownedthesmallwellstockedsweetshopinportscathoeachsummerholidaywe

wouldrushdownthecobbledstreetsfightingtogettherefirstmorningboyshedmutteras

weclamberedtochooseoursweets

_____

_____

_____

_____

_____

_____

_____

○ 16

List each word class these words are in.

D 6

92 relieve   _____   **93** religion   _____

94 related   _____   **95** really   _____

4

E 2

Rewrite these words correctly.

96 condem   _____

97 sychology   _____

98 morgage   _____

99 garantee   _____

100 gourme   _____

5

Now go to the Progress Chart to record your score!   Total   100

Act 1 Scene 1

Enter Denis

DENIS	Calls your worship?
OLIVER	Was not Charles, the Duke's wrestler, here to speak with me?
DENIS	So please you, he is here at the door, and importunes access to you.
OLIVER	Call him in.
	'Twill be a good way. And tomorrow the wrestling is.

5

Enter Charles

CHARLES	Good morrow to your worship.
OLIVER	Good Monsieur Charles – what's the new news at the new court?
CHARLES	There's no news at the court, sir, but the old news: that is, the old Duke is banished by his younger brother, the new Duke, and three or four loving lords have put themselves into voluntary exile with him, whose lands and revenues enrich the new Duke; therefore he gives them good leave to wander.
OLIVER	Can you tell if Rosalind, the Duke's daughter, be banished with her father?
CHARLES	O no; for the Duke's daughter her cousin so loves her, being ever from their cradles bred together, that she would have followed her exile, or have died to stay behind her. She is at the court, and no less beloved of her uncle than his own daughter; and never two ladies loved as they do.
OLIVER	Where will the old Duke live?

10

15

20

CHARLES   They say he is already in the forest of Ardenne, and a many merry
           men with him; and there they live like the old Robin Hood of England.
           They say many young gentlemen flock to him every day, and fleet the
           time carelessly, as they did in the golden world.   25
[*Oliver and Charles then continue to talk about the wrestling at some length.
They both exit.*]

Act 1 Scene 2

Enter Rosalind and Celia

CELIA   I pray thee Rosalind, sweet my coz, be merry.   30
ROSALIND   Dear Celia, I show more mirth than I am mistress of; and would you yet
           I were merrier? Unless you could teach me to forget a banished father
           you must not learn me how to remember any extraordinary pleasure.
CELIA   Herein I see thou lovest me not with the full weight that I love thee. If
           my uncle, thy banished father, had banished thy uncle, the Duke my   35
           father, so thou hadst been still with me I could have taught my love to
           take thy father for mine. So wouldst thou, if the truth of thy love to me
           were so righteously tempered as mine is to thee.
ROSALIND   Well, I will forget the condition of my estate to rejoice in yours.
CELIA   You know my father hath no child but I, nor none is like to have. And   40
           truly, when he dies thou shalt be his heir; for what he hath taken
           away from thy father perforce, I will render thee again in affection. By
           mine honour I will, and when I break that oath, let me turn monster.
           Therefore, my sweet Rose, my dear Rose, be merry.
ROSALIND   From henceforth I will, coz, and devise sports.   45
           Let me see, what think you of falling in love?
                                        From *As You Like It* by William Shakespeare

Answer these questions.

   1 Who is the servant, Denis or Oliver? _____

   2 What is Charles's occupation? _____

   3 Write the words in the passage that mean 'wants to meet you'.

   _____

   4–5 Give two reasons why Oliver is keen to speak to Charles.

   _____

   _____

   6 What family relationship does the old Duke have with the new Duke?

   _____

7 Why was Rosalind not banished with her father the old Duke?

_____

_____

8 The new Duke didn't stop the lords leaving. Why?

_____

_____

9 Why is reference made to Robin Hood?

_____

_____

10 What is meant by the **phrase** 'flock to him every day' (line 24)?

_____

11 What is the purpose of the information presented in italics?

_____

12 What is troubling Rosalind in lines 32 to 33? ('Unless you could teach me… remember any extraordinary pleasure.')

_____

_____

13 The word 'coz' is used in line 30. Of what is this an **abbreviation**?

_____

14 What does the word 'mirth' mean (line 31)? _____

15 Why does Celia believe that she loves Rosalind more than Rosalind loves her?

_____

_____

16 What does Celia promise to do for Rosalind when her father, the new duke, dies?

_____

_____

17 What does Celia mean when she says 'let me turn monster' (line 43)?

_____

_____

18–19 What are two possible reasons Celia calls Rosalind 'Rose'?

_____

_____

20 What does Rosalind promise to do in her last line?

_____

_____

20

D 5

Add the missing apostrophes.

21 the farmers chicken coop   **22** the six ducks eggs

23 the last fledglings mother   **24** the twelve lions cubs

25 the old ponys reins   **26** the three cats muddy paws

6

E 2

Match each word with its **definition** in bold by writing the correct number in the space.

     (1) child   (2) hill   (3) tranquil   (4) release

     (5) joking   (6) pick   (7) buy   (8) cease

27 calm   _____   **28** jocular   _____

29 purchase   _____   **30** bairn   _____

31 detach   _____   **32** stop   _____

33 pluck   _____   **34** tor   _____

8

D 6

State whether each of these **sentences** has an **active** or **passive verb**.

35 The terrified mouse was chased by the cat. _____

36 Jeremy poured the water into a bucket. _____

37 My arm was bitten by the fierce dog. _____

38 The child was knocked over by the speeding car. _____

39 A branch broke and fell to the ground. _____

40 Tom knocked over the goldfish bowl. _____

6

Write a **definition** for each of these expressions.

E 2

41 to turn over a new leaf _____

42 every cloud has a silver lining _____

43 to sit on the fence _____

44 waste not want not _____

45 a bolt from the blue _____

46 to call a spade a spade _____ 6

Make up your own **mnemonic** for each of these words.

E 2

47 separate _____

_____

48 argument _____

_____

49 continuous _____

_____

50 perseverance _____

_____ 4

Add a different **conjunction** to complete each **sentence**.

D 2

51 They went to Switzerland _____ there was plenty of snow.

52 Will you come for a walk _____ do you want to watch television?

53 The playground will be much safer _____ it is resurfaced.

54 Let's eat our lunch _____ we wait for the train. 4

Write a statement and a question that include the words in bold.

D 1

55–56 **weather   tree   road**

Statement _____

Question _____

57–58 cancelled   Spain   today

Statement _____

Question _____

59–60 lost   young   rain

Statement _____

Question _____

61–62 test   relieved   result

Statement _____

Question _____ ◯ **8**

⬡ E 2

Complete these **similes**.

63 as quiet as a _____

64 as strong as an _____

65 as silent as the _____

66 as cold as _____

67 as bright as a _____

68 as hard as _____ ◯ **6**

⬡ E 2

Rewrite these words correctly.

69 goverment _____	70 liason _____
71 Febuary _____	72 acommodation _____
73 tranquility _____	74 supercede _____
75 conveniance _____	76 advertisment _____
77 iminent _____	78 extravegant _____

◯ **10**

58

Add the missing commas in the passage.

D 4

79–84 They walked home again there being nothing more of interest to see. As they came in through the front-door of the big house the first thing Tom heard was the ticking of the grandfather clock. It would tick on to bedtime and in that way Time was Tom's friend; but after that it would tick on to Saturday and in that way Time was Tom's enemy.

From Tom's Midnight Garden by Philippa Pearce

6

From each of the words in bold make an **adjective** to fit the sentence.

D 6

85 humour   The _____ comedian was very entertaining.

86 hunger   The _____ children grabbed at the food.

87 disaster   The audience was unimpressed by the _____ performance.

88 rely   The Jacobs' 1960s car was still _____ .

4

Change these formal **sentences** to informal **sentences**.

D 1

89 The lesson is about to commence.

_____

90 I willl endeavour to do my best.

_____

91 Might I suggest you leave early?

_____

92 Shall I come to your house or alternatively you could come to mine?

_____

4

Write what you think each **prefix** means and then write a word with that **prefix**.

E 2

93–94 hex =   _____   _____

95–96 circum =   _____   _____

97–98 micro =   _____   _____

99–100 il =   _____   _____

8

I'd impetuously said I would stay for three nights when I booked into my hotel, and
by mid-morning of the third day I was beginning to feel a little restless, so I decided
to have a walk to Sutton Courtenay for no reason other than George Orwell is
buried there and it seemed about the right distance. I walked out of the city by way
of a water meadow to North Hinksey and onwards towards Boar's Hill through 5
an area called, with curious indecisiveness, Chilswell Valley or Happy Valley. It had
rained in the night and the heavy clay soil stuck to my boots and made the going
arduous. Soon I had an accumulation of mud that doubled the size of my feet. A bit
further on the path had been covered with loose chippings, presumably to make the
going easier, but in fact the chippings stuck to my muddy boots so that it looked as 10
if I were walking around with two very large currant buns on my feet…

Sutton Courtenay seemed considerably further on than I recalled it from the map,
but it was a pleasant walk with frequent views of the Thames. It is a charming place,
with some fine homes, three agreeable-looking pubs, and a little green with a war
memorial, beside which stands the churchyard where not only George Orwell 15
lies, but also H.H. Asquith. Call me a perennial Iowa farmboy, but I never fail to be
impressed by how densely packed with worthies is this little island. How remarkable
it is that in a single village churchyard you find the graves of two men of global
stature. We in Iowa would be proud of either of them – indeed we would be proud
of Trigger the Wonder Horse or the guy who invented traffic cones or pretty much 20
anyone at all.

I walked into the graveyard and found Orwell's grave. It had three straggly rose
bushes growing out of it and some artificial flowers in a glass jar, before a simple
stone with a curiously terse inscription:

Here lies Eric Arthur Blair 25
Born June 25th 1903
Died January 21st 1950

Not much sentiment there, what? Near by was the grave of Herbert Henry Asquith.
It was one of those tea-caddy tombs, and it was sinking into the ground in an
alarming manner. His inscription too was mysteriously to the point. It said simply: 30

Earl of Oxford and Asquith
Prime Minister of England
April 1908 to December 1916
Born 12 September 1852
Died 15 February 1928 35

Notice anything odd there? I bet you did if you are Scottish or Welsh. The whole
place was a bit strange. I mean to say here was a cemetery containing the grave of
a famous author that was made as anonymous as if he had been buried a pauper,
and another of a man whose descendants had apparently forgotten exactly what he
was Prime Minister of and which looked seriously in danger of being swallowed by 40
the earth.

From *Notes from a Small Island* by Bill Bryson

Answer these questions.

1 Why did Bill Bryson decide to go to Sutton Courtenay?

_____

2 Why did the author believe that Chilswell Valley had been named indecisively?

_____

3 Which river did Bill Bryson often see? _____

4 What is the nationality of the author? _____

5–6 On line 17 which island is Bill referring to? Why does he call it little?

_____

_____

7 What is meant by 'two men of global stature' (lines 18–19)?

_____

8 Was George Orwell alive at the same time as Asquith? _____

9 What do you notice about the inscription on George Orwell's grave?

_____

_____

10 What is Bill Bryson referring to when he asks 'Notice anything odd there?' (line 36)?

_____

_____

11–13 Give the meaning of the following words as they are used in the passage:

'impetuously' (line 1) _____

'terse' (line 24) _____

'anonymous' (line 38) _____

14–15 Do you get the impression that Iowa has many famous people buried there? Use evidence to support your answer.

_____

_____

_____

_____

16–17 Find two examples from the passage that highlight Bill Bryson's sense of humour.

_____

_____

_____

18–20 Imagine Bill Bryson has been asked whether Sutton Courtenay is worth a visit by some friends who are later touring the area. He e-mails his response. Write below the e-mail Bill writes to them.

_____

_____

_____

_____

_____

_____

_____

_____

◯ 20

E 2

Match and add a word that originated from each country.

	spaghetti	pyjamas	encore	movie

21–22 America   _____   _____

23–24 France   _____   _____

25–26 Italy   _____   _____

27–28 India   _____   _____

◯ 8

In each space, write the **superlative** form of the word in bold.

29 **good**   This is the _____ party I have ever been to.

30 **long**   The _____ road is in the Pennines.

31 **many**   _____ of you have brought your wellingtons.

32 **tasty**   Your mince pies are the _____ I have ever had.

33 **wonderful**   It was quite the _____ place I have ever visited.

34 **little**   Be very quiet! Make the _____ noise possible.

35 **bad**   It was the _____ storm for many years.   7

Copy these **sentences**, adding an **adjectival phrase** to improve each one.

36 Mr Trump chased the children out of his garden.

_____

37 The school netball team won the cup.

_____

38 The dogs ran towards the sheep.

_____

39 The Walker family watched the sun set over the hill.

_____

40 George's sailing boat capsized in the sea.

_____   5

Write the name of the person that 'fits' the word on the left.

Example   consult   *consultant*

41 advertise   _____   42 music   _____

43 absent   _____   44 admire   _____

45 assist   _____   46 cash   _____

47 imitate   _____   48 magic   _____

49 teach   _____   50 compete _____   10

Write an **onomatopoeic** word for each object.

51 cork   _____   52 drum   _____

53 clock   _____   54 water   _____

55 whip   _____   56 coins   _____

Write each of these hyphenated words correctly in a **sentence**.

57 hand-made   _____

58 long-distance   _____

59 record-breaking   _____

60 short-sleeved   _____

Write a different **adverb** to complete each **sentence**.

61 The burglar crept _____.

62 The child answered _____.

63 The boy coughed _____.

64 The athlete finished _____.

Write a short argument, including the words/**phrases** in bold, that explains your opinions about whether boxing should be banned.

65–72	**viewpoint**	**conclusion**	**opinion**
	furthermore	**as well as**	**believe**
	contention	**although**	

_____

_____

_____

_____

_____

_____

_____

_____

Add a **prefix** and **suffix** to each of these **root words**.

Example   believe   **un**believ**able**

73 press   _____   74 happy   _____

75 lock   _____   76 agree   _____

77 turn   _____   78 take   _____

79 operate   _____   80 do   _____

Copy this passage, adding the missing punctuation.

81–100 As Monty raced off down the beach, Brian and Jess began to feel a little concerned Monty was a lovely black Labrador who was a little unreliable when it came to listening to commands Monty come back called Jess Weve got to go home But Monty seemed not to hear He put his nose down to the sand picked up a scent of something good and was off

You'd better wait here I'll chase after him suggested Brian beginning to feel annoyed with his disobedient dog.

_____

_____

_____

_____

_____

_____

_____

_____

_____

_____

Progress Chart   English 11⁺–12⁺ years Book 2

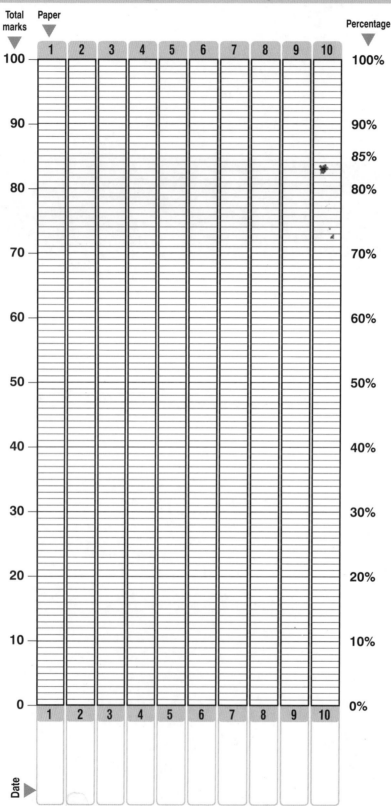

Total marks ▼

Paper ▼

| | 1 | 2 | 3 | 4 | 5 | 6 | 7 | 8 | 9 | 10 |

Percentage ▼

100 — 100%

90 — 90%

85%

80 — 80%

70 — 70%

60 — 60%

50 — 50%

40 — 40%

30 — 30%

20 — 20%

10 — 10%

0 — 0%

| | 1 | 2 | 3 | 4 | 5 | 6 | 7 | 8 | 9 | 10 |

Date ▶

When you've finished the book use the Next Steps Planner ▶